Bristol Under Siege

Bristol Under Siege

Surviving the Wartime Blitz

Compiled and written by

Helen Reid

 redcliffe

First published in 2005 by Redcliffe Press Ltd.,
81g Pembroke Road, Bristol BS8 3EA

ISBN 1 904537 25 1

British Library Cataloguing-in-Publication Data
A catalogue record for this book is available from the British Library

Design and typesetting by Stephen Morris Communications:
smc@freeuk.com Bristol and Liverpool.

Printed by HSW Print, Tonypandy, Rhondda.

above: Palmyra Road, Bedminster. A scene replicated throughout the city
title page: A surreal scene in Park Street

Contents

FOREWORD

This book has been compiled from several Redcliffe Press accounts of Bristol in wartime: *Bristol Blitz Diary*, John Dike, 1982; *Bristol Blitz: The Untold Story*, Helen Reid, 1988; *Siren Nights*, republished 1989; *Target Filton*, Kenneth Wakefield, 1990, and *West at War*, James Belsey and Helen Reid, 1990. Many of the interviews in *West at War* were conducted by Testimony Films for the television documentary which accompanied the book.

Useful references are: *The Air Defence of the Bristol Area*, Bristol Historical Association, pamphlet No. 90; *Bristol at War*, Prof. C M MacInnes, Museum Press, 1962; *Bristol Blitzed*, photographs collected by Reece Winstone, 1973; *Bristol Bombed*, photographs G Warne, 1943; *Joyce's War,* Joyce Storey, Bristol Broadsides, 1990; *Luftwaffe Operations over Bristol*, Bristol Historical Association, pamphlet No. 85.

Some of the most striking images of the Second World War were the work of the outstanding Bristol photo-journalist Jim Facey.

Jim joined the staff of the *Evening Post*'s predecessor, the *Bristol Times & Echo*, as a boy. After the paper was closed down, Jim was one of the chosen few invited to set up the *Evening Post* in 1932. When the Second World War broke out, Jim was the *Post*'s picture editor and chief photographer. He showed skill, flair and considerable bravery, often leaving the relative safety of air raid shelters to photograph the raids as they happened. He realised that many of his war-time pictures would never be published at the time. They were too strong, too emotive to pass the censor's scrutiny, but that did not deter him. He took the pictures anyway.

He was so well known on Bristol's war-time scene that when Queen Mary, the then Queen Mother, spotted him and he failed to notice her, she gave him a cheerful prod in the back with her umbrella. 'Come on, Jim,' she called out, 'get on with your work.'

Jim Facey's pictures have a rare quality. Besides documenting the damage and the nightmare quality of a city under fire, they also emphasise the plight of ordinary people caught up in a great conflict, the women and children who suffered as well as the volunteers who did so much to help the victims. He died in 1977.

My thanks to *Bristol Evening Post* for the use of most of the photographs in this book.

Glossary

Ack-ack: anti-aircraft guns

AFS: Auxiliary Fire Service

Alert: the Air Raid Warning, a siren with a swooping up and down note

All Clear: the single high note that indicated an air raid was over

ARP: Air Raid Precautions, supervised by Air Raid Wardens in each area

HE: High Explosive

UXB: Unexploded bomb

Girls unaware that their days spent window-shopping in the old city are numbered

INTRODUCTION

It would be presumptuous to claim that Bristol's experience in the front line during the Second World War matched the sufferings of Leningrad under siege. The scale of death and destruction was infinitely greater in the heroic Russian city. Nevertheless, Bristolians could empathise with the inhabitants, for they too had suffered a siege of their own.

Leningrad was under siege from September 1941 to February 1943, but before that Bristol had been under siege for almost a year, from June 1940 through a bitter winter until April 1941, and had experienced the same physical and psychological damage, the same fears and hopes, the same courage and despair while under attack. In both cities, lives were scarred for ever.

As in Leningrad, though on a much smaller scale, Bristol suffered shortages, power cuts, hunger and sickness, and lowered morale; both cities kept their civic pride, and defended their home town, sometimes to the death. In both, citizens performed acts of amazing bravery and endurance under attack. As in Leningrad, the people of Bristol had to watch a much loved historic city being systematically destroyed.

Like Leningrad, Bristol was not properly prepared for attack, and its people lived under constant fear of bombardment, so much so that some fled to the countryside every night, and sheltered in ditches, while others sought refuge in the city's caves and tunnels to escape the relentless German bombardment.

For Bristol during that siege year was the fourth most bombed city in Britain. It was an obvious target, with its docks and aircraft industry and, even when proper defences were in place, the Luftwaffe could always find its way to the city, for there was no way of camouflaging the waterway that led to its heart.

Night after night the bombs fell, and by the end of the conflict, after 548 raids, the final reckoning was grim: 1,229 people were killed, 3,305 were injured, 3,000 homes were destroyed and many thousands more damaged. The old business and commercial heart of the city had become a vast heap of rubble, ancient landmarks had gone for ever. Bristol's historic skyline had been smashed, and for the older generation who remember the lost city the sorrow still goes on.

And it was not the first time the city had suffered under siege, for from 1643 to 1645

Wine Street in 1936. Christ Church is one of the few buildings in this picture to survive the Blitz. Everything in the foreground was destroyed

... and an earlier photograph of a busy Castle Street

Bristol was in the thick of the Civil War, and came under attack from both Roundheads and Royalists as the city changed hands in the fortunes of battle.

That earlier war is long forgotten, but the Second World War is well documented, and has been mythologised over the years. *Bristol under Siege* is the real story of how Bristol coped with the horrors of saturation bombing from the air, and told by those who lived through those terrible, exciting times. Some wrote contemporary accounts, others remembered their unforgettable experiences fifty or more years on.

What saved Bristol was the subject of this blitz poem, by the late Rev. Paul Shipley:

Resilience

I stood on the brow of a smouldering hill,
And gazed on a city a thousand years old;
It lay at my feet in an ocean of fire,
Writhing in agony, tested as gold

in a furnace. Her churches 'midst torturing flames
Stood guarding, like sentinels, her proud, unbowed soul,
Symbols of things which naught can destroy –
Love, mercy, truth, justice; Man's faith in his goal.

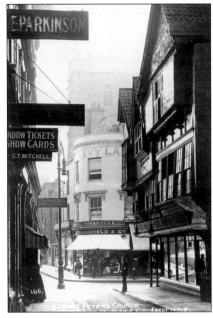

An atmospheric St Mary-le-Port Street. Only the ruins of the church are to be seen today. The fine timbered building on the right was lost to commercial vandalism in the 1930s before Hitler's bombs could do their worst

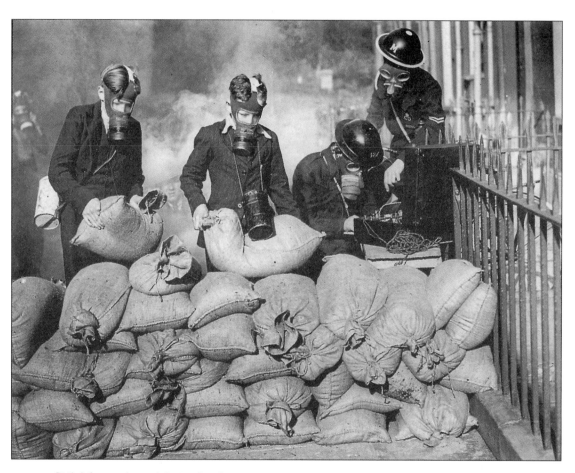

Civil defence rehearsal during the phoney war

THE SIEGE BEGINS SEPTEMBER 25, 1940

CHAPTER ONE

Like the rest of Britain, Bristol marked time during the so-called phoney war that lasted from September 3, 1939, until the first raid on the city on June 20, 1940. Civil defences were slowly put in place, refugees from London arrived in Bristol and the West country, which were then considered safe areas. Shelters were dug, the blackout curtains were put up and everyone waited. Rationing started early in 1940 and people got used to air-raid rehearsals, carrying gas masks, queues, weak beer and invasion rumours.

But Bristol was not ready for siege. At the start of the war there were 3,500 public shelter places available, when the Home Office calculated that 25,000 were needed. Many of the shelters were defective and collapsed because the wrong mortar had been used. The supply of Anderson shelters for back gardens was sporadic; Bristol was waiting for another 800 to be delivered when the first raids began.

The Fire Service was under strength; at the first big raid on the city, when over 400 appliances were needed, only 224 were available – the rest had broken down or were incomplete. The regular Fire Brigade was short of 77 men. Only 50 of the 200 ambulances required were available.

The bubble of security burst with the fall of France in June, and then the arrival of some of the shattered survivors of Dunkirk at Temple Meads railway station. The first air raid on Bristol was a flop, with a few bombs falling on the shingle at Portishead, and then the first raid to cause deaths came on June 25, when five were killed, but there were few serious raids that summer. Then came Bristol's wake-up call: the raid on Filton, on September 25, 1940. Although Bristol did

May 10, 1940:
more ominous news

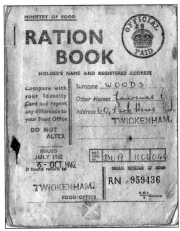

The household food
allowance was
imposed in 1940

Air raid shelter on College Green, 1939

not know it, its siege had begun.

The city was an inevitable target. As well as the Bristol Aeroplane Company at Filton, there was Parnall's the shopfitters which had turned to making aircraft components, there was Gardiners, the iron founders, now making gun mounts, rocket-launcher bases and torpedo cases; Sheldon Bush was producing ammunition, Strachan and Henshaw were making submarine detection equipment, trench mortar bombs and anti-aircraft shells, while Butler Oil made pitch for aerodrome runways and explosives. And the docks in Bristol, Avonmouth and Portishead were taking in vital supplies and sending out these products of Bristol's war effort. Everyone knew Bristol was for it – the question was when.

Home Guard demonstrations in Queen Square

When the wailing up-and-down sound of the siren went on September 25, no one was very alarmed. Arthur Backhurst was working at BAC, Filton, that day. 'When the siren went, we just ambled to the shelters, thinking we'd have half an hour off and then go back to work again. There was never any sort of urgency then.'

But in broad daylight a perfect Y-shaped formation of 58 Heinkel bombers, escorted by 40 Messerschmitt fighters, had flown across the Channel, and over Dorset and Somerset virtually unchallenged.

The daylight raid on Filton was a turning point in the West's war. The simple statistics were these: 350 bombs fell in an area roughly one mile square, damaging not only the works severely, but 900 Filton and Patchway houses, and the railway line. Inside the

Surveying Bristol's aerial defences

factory complex, 72 were killed and 166 injured, of whom 19 later died. Outside the works, 58 died and 154 were seriously injured, and 11 soldiers lost their lives as they marched along the road. Those are the bald facts, but what happened that day remained indelibly etched on the minds of people who were there, like Arthur Backhurst:

Well, the sirens went between twenty and ten to twelve, so we locked our tool boxes and got together in groups and just ambled to the surface shelters. We started to play cards. We'd been in there about a quarter of an hour when someone came running down the shelter saying 'this one's got our number on it', and sure enough there was this terrible whistle and bang, and when it banged you had this compression feeling. I was actually lying on the blast, ten feet above the ground, I could see Patchway burning, and then I came down with a bang and one wall of the shelter fell on me and on some of my work-mates, and we were trapped. We were in there a good hour until they got us out. At that stage I thought my feet had gone, I couldn't feel them. I was shouting 'Get me out of here' and the man on my left was dead, and the man on my right was dead.

Fred Caple was in a different shelter:

I remember we just strolled from the fac-tory floor, hundreds of us, and as we went to the shelters we looked up and there was this glittering, like tinfoil in the sky, something shining, dropping down, thousands of sheets of it… and then we all made a dive because we could actual-ly see the bombs leaving the aircraft. We were jammed in, the bombs were raining down and we were literally being lifted inches off the floor with the blast. We could hear the clattering of the cars which were being blown on top of the shelter. I was only 19 at the time and I shall never forget it: it seemed to me that some of the older people were mumbling the Lord's Prayer.

We were all on the floor, all on top of one another, but none of us was hit. We all got out somehow and all I could think of was getting home. So I rushed out to the main gate and came upon the worst scene I've ever seen. I was literally stepping

Destination Filton:
enemy bombers flying in deadly formation

over bodies, they were being stacked up against the railings outside the works and the blood was running down the road. The bodies were of soldiers who had been marching from the Rodney works to Patchway at the time, and after the carnage I saw I went home and was sick. It took a long time to heal me from that sight.

Though security was tight on the Filton raid, with so many people involved word got around the city. Gerald Smith, who in peace time worked at BAC, later said:

Even today, not everything's been told about that raid. It's very difficult to glean any information from the survivors. And to this day I've never been able to find where the bombs actually fell. In 21 years working at the company, nobody could point to where it all happened. People just wanted to forget it.

The high death toll among BAC employees was mainly caused by a series of direct hits by high-explosive bombs on six crowded air raid shelters, and upon arrival rescue and first aid personnel were confronted with terrible scenes. Some shelters had caved in, burying their occupants, while others were blasted wide open, the craters revealing bodies mutilated and dismembered by the violence of the explosions. Distinguishing the dead from the dying or badly injured was a task not readily forgotten by those to whom this duty fell.

There were countless examples of bravery among those at the receiving end of the bombing that day, but few endured more than fifty-year-old Mrs. Alice Peacock. Shortly after the factory warning she was sitting in No. 1 Shelter with some friends, most of whom were talking or knitting, when there was a tremendous explosion. Mrs. Peacock was found some distance away, covered by débris and trapped by her legs, but still conscious. About three hours later, during which time she was given pain-relieving drugs, she was released and taken to hospital in Bristol with many other injured BAC employees.

Alice Peacock was not traced by her family until mid-afternoon the next day, when they discovered that she was alive but had lost both legs. She eventually mastered the use of artificial limbs and returned to her home in Bishopston. When fully recovered she resumed her war work at Filton, an unsung heroine surely deserving of recognition. And she was by no means alone in her courage and steadfastness.

Bomb damage: German reconnaissance photograph of Filton, September 27 1940

As reported by the German crews, most of the ninety tons of high explosives and all 24 oil bombs landed on or around the target. In total 168 bombs were counted within the factory area, extensively damaging the Rodney Works and causing many casualties at the Flight Shed and East Engine Works, where the six shelters were hit. The main aircraft assembly halls were hit and severely damaged and two of the five buildings concerned with engine manufacture were damaged; one building was almost totally destroyed by fire and the roof of another was shattered. Eight newly built aircraft were destroyed and another twenty-four were damaged. Machine tools suffered badly, both by bombing and by the effects of water when some mains were fractured, and further

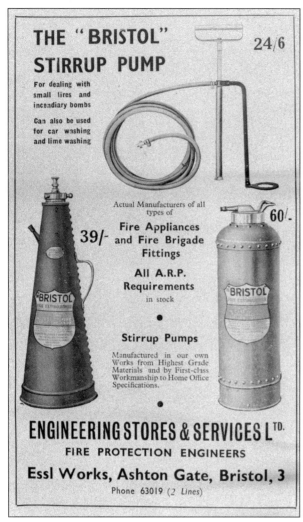
Bristol's own defence against incendiary attacks

water damage was caused by the factory sprinkler system. In the factory car parks numerous vehicles were damaged and many were burnt out.

The large number of people killed and injured made notification of next-of-kin and the identification of bodies very difficult. Filton Church was pressed into use as a temporary mortuary and an excellent job was done by company welfare officers and others who made innumerable visits to bereaved relatives and others. Apart from the personal tragedies the war effort also suffered, for among those killed were valuable technical staff who proved difficult to replace in a highly specialised industry.

While works' firemen strove to extinguish the fires that resulted, assistance was rushed to Filton by the Bristol ARP and the Fire Services. Scenes of sheer chaos greeted them upon arrival. Buildings and vehicles burned furiously in a smoke-filled, dust-laden atmosphere while stunned survivors, many of whom had miraculous escapes from death or serious injury, made their way over rubble-strewn roads within the factory complex. Rescue attempts were seriously hampered by a large number of delayed action or 'dud' bombs that were scattered far and wide; of twenty ambulances sent to Filton seven were damaged by bombs which exploded after the attack. The delayed action bombs also caused nine casualties among first-aid and medical personnel.

Efforts to make good the damage at Filton and at the Rodney Works and Patchway met with a degree of success that exceeded all expectations. The speed with which electricity was restored, for example, was typical, the current being reinstated within five hours. This was a magnificent effort that was applauded by Lord Beaverbrook, the Minister for Aircraft Production, when he visited the factory a few days later.

One effect of the raid that the Germans could not determine was the remarkable change it produced upon the civilian population. Until now, with bombing of a generally desultory nature, few people seemed to have feelings against Germany that could be termed close to hatred but now, with many homes in and around Bristol mourning the loss of relatives and friends, feelings hardened. Despite the generally acknowledged legitimacy of the target there was a new loathing of the Nazis, as all Germans were then termed, and especially of 'Nazi airmen'. This strengthened still further the determination to resist the enemy, no matter what,

Government advertisement encouraging Britons to grow their own food

and indirectly fortified the civil population against heavier and much more destructive attacks that were yet to come. But all of this was in the future and it was the present that occupied the thoughts of the people at Filton when, at 12.16, the sirens sounded the long, steady note of the All Clear for, although the raiders had departed, the task of retrieving the bodies of the dead and tending the wounds of the injured was just beginning.

Rescue work and the clearing of roads blocked by rubble had barely got under way when, about an hour after the All Clear, the sirens again brought work to a halt. This time, however, the intruder was only a high-flying enemy reconnaissance aircraft bent on photographing the results of the attack.

Elizabeth Craig's *Cooking in War-time*:
'I'll take no excuse for a want of variey in meals.'

Throughout the rest of the day, and for much of the next, explosions continued to rock the Filton district as delayed-action bombs detonated. Word of the disaster at the factory spread throughout Bristol and its environs and the homecoming of employees was awaited with trepidation. In many cases the fears were groundless but for others the previously distant horrors of total warfare became a close and tragic reality.

Bristol, shaken and angry at the ease with which Luftwaffe pilots were able to fly in immaculate formation over the Dorset coast and make straight for Bristol claimed there was a gap in the ack-ack defences. So in September 1940 Alderman Frank Parrish, chairman of the Emergency Committee, paid a top-secret visit to Ernest Bevin, Minister of Labour, to complain, and within a week the gap in the city's ground defences had been filled with four of the most modern anti-aircraft guns available.

The truth was that Bristol was very weakly defended, which was inevitable in view of the many years of neglect that had preceded the war and the terrible strain which was at that time placed upon the Royal Air Force by the determined attack of the enemy. No British planes had appeared in the skies of Bristol that morning, and few people paused to ask the reason why. So they indulged in much understandable but unreasonable anger. Fortunately, no one in the city then knew the insignificant number of British fighters which still remained to oppose the enemy.

The instant protests had their effect; when the Luftwaffe came back to bomb BAC the second time on September 27 they were met by RAF Hurricanes, and there were no casualties. But the Filton raid had shaken people's confidence. Maybe this war was not going to be easy to win.

And the effect on that all-important morale was significant. Arthur Backhurst, recovered from the injury to his feet, went back to work at BAC a fortnight after leaving hospital:

> I went to my place and I cried because all my workmates had gone and there were strangers in their place. There were only about two millers left out of thirteen. It was devastating. I looked at the empty machines and the tears just ran down my face. I stood it all morning and then I went to the superintendent, and I was nearly in tears. He said 'Can't you stand it, lad?' and I said 'No, I don't think I can.' So he sent and got my cards and my wages and I just left.

That daylight raid on Filton on September 25, 1940, had come as a stark reminder that Britain was no longer an isolated island, that the seas which had protected us throughout our history were no defence against air attack and that the West Country was all too vulnerable. The Luftwaffe had lost the Battle of Britain, now it was turning its attention to wreaking a terrible vengeance on the British people with a night-time bombing campaign that quickly introduced a chilling, menacing new word into everyday language – the Blitz. The great raids on London began in September 1940. By mid-November the bombers were ranging further afield to the major provincial cities. Coventry was the first to experience the horrors, then Southampton, then Birmingham. When would it be Bristol's turn?

Bristol had faced its first real baptism of fire at Filton, and already nerves were stretched too tight. But far worse was to come, as the Luftwaffe set out for Bristol on November 24...

Dolphin Street, from the corner of Peter Street

A BAPTISM OF FIRE NOVEMBER 24 TO 25, 1940

CHAPTER TWO

When the city's 338th alert of the war was sounded at 6.22 p.m. on Sunday, November 24, no one took a great deal of notice. They had heard the alarms far too often to believe they warned of any great danger. It had been a quiet, dull, November Sunday.

Across the English Channel it had been foggy earlier in the day, grounding the Luftwaffe's fleet of 214 long-range bombers at their bases on the northern coast of France. But as the afternoon wore on, so the fog began to clear. The bombers could set out once more. There was a hint that conditions might become foggy once more later in the night, so the tacticians decided to limit operations to the first half of the night, choosing targets which would allow the crews ample time to return by midnight. The evening's priority: to eliminate Bristol as an important port supplying much of the Midlands and the south of England.

A fleet of 134 bombers took off to smash the heart of Bristol. The attack was to follow the by now well established pattern perfected by the German air crews in their operations over London and elsewhere. The most experienced crews would be in the vanguard, dropping flares to pinpoint the target for their comrades. Then came showers of incendiary bombs, easily extinguishable with sand or earth, water or even the stamp of a heavy boot, but lethal in their sheer weight of numbers as they lit more and more fires, causing havoc and terror as they fell in tens of thousands. And then came the HEs, the devastatingly powerful high explosive bombs designed to rip apart buildings, shatter mains services, destroy roads and railways and disrupt fire-fighting supplies and communications. This lethal assault would leave the target in blazing chaos, a brilliantly lit beacon for the less experienced crews to attack in later waves.

The science fiction fantasy had been of a well drilled, close-flying fleet which would arrive in perfect formation, rapidly destroy and fly home, and that had, indeed, been the pattern of the tactical assault on Filton. But when it came to the strategic bombing of Britain's cities, another plan was brought into operation. This assault was even more unbearable for its victims, a hellish, seemingly endless column of enemy aircraft which came singly and at intervals of two of three minutes for hour after hour, shattering nerves and destroying hope with its sheer, inexorable relentlessness.

Not entirely wishful thinking: a Messerschmitt AG advertisement, depicting the hoped-for success of the Bf 110 fighter-bomber

All of that was to come that dull November evening. Bristol had been going about its lazy, Sunday business. The city centre was quiet but not deserted. Religious services were attracting large congregations at churches and halls and there were plenty of families and individuals who had been spending the day with friends or relatives and who were now making their way across the central areas by foot or on the reduced weekend bus and tram services.

Gladys Locke and her husband were at the Colston Hall, the large concert hall just off Bristol's city centre. There was always the risk of an air raid, but Bristol had seemed so peaceful and they enjoyed the Sunday night religious services. Gladys was expecting their child:

My husband said, 'It's pretty safe, I don't think there'll be anything tonight,' because we hadn't had any attacks for nights. So we went to the Colston Hall and we'd just got there, we were sat quite close to the organ.

I asked my husband, 'What's that noise?' It was bombs being dropped. And they announced that a raid had actually started. There was a bit of a panic and everybody tried to get out. But they wouldn't let anybody out. We sheltered under the organ and I went hysterical. A nurse came along and you know the old-fashioned way of dealing with hysterical people. She gave me a slap across the face. I wanted to get home to my mum because I knew she would be absolutely terrified... I was going to have a baby and I was trying to protect my baby and go and see my mother and, oh, it was terrible.

Castle Street on the morning after: November 25, 1940. The Regent Cinema Café sign still reads 'Open daily 11am-10pm'

The first moments of the raid had transformed a blacked-out Bristol. One minute there had been darkness, the next the falling parachute flares lit up the city with a ghostly silver-white brilliance as the air hummed with the heavy drone of enemy bombers making their run-ins at 13,000 feet.

Bob Chappell had been visiting his parents in Easton when the alarm was raised and he was keen to get back to his own family as quickly as possible. His wife had given birth to their second daughter only seven days before and he didn't want to leave her alone. He walked to Castle Street:

> So I walked up to Halfords, facing the Regent cinema, and as I stood in Halfords' doorway I could look through the glass doors of the Regent and suddenly I saw fire starting in the foyer. I thought I'd better get the hell out of there so I went past St Peter's Hospital and turned left into Bridge Street and

Park Street, November 25, 1940

then suddenly I heard an almighty bang from an HE. When I got down to the bottom of Bridge Street I could see that one side of the bridge was out and I could see an army of rats walking across the bridge. The only thing missing was the Pied Piper standing in front.

I walked over Bristol Bridge and when I turned into Redcliffe Street I could see one tramcar on its side, one tramcar standing up straight on the rails and then behind that, about 50 yards further on, was another tramcar on its side and all the overhead wires were down. So I picked my way gingerly over the wires, not knowing whether they were live or dead. Eventually I got to St. Mary Redcliffe Church. It was like daylight with all the fires. There were two surface shelters there so I entered one and pulled the sacking aside that acted

Firefighters in the remains of Wine Street

like a curtain. There were two blokes sitting there scrapping and I asked what it was it all about? One of them told me, 'This silly bugger here was striking matches, and with an air raid on.' I said, 'Come and look outside. If you've today's *News of the World* you can put a chair outside and read it.' There were two girls there about 17 or 18, and they were breaking their hearts because they'd been caught in the raid. So I had a chat with them and we all sat down together.

Irene Crew and her husband had been reunited the day before when he had returned home on leave from the navy. They were staying in a house near Castle Street when the air raid warning went. They hurried next door to their neighbour's shelter. Nearby was a brewery with a wine and spirit store and stables for the dray horses. Soon the air was thick with the sound of whistling, falling bombs, of the patter of countless incendiaries landing, of the thump and crash of HEs exploding and of the bangs of anti-aircraft guns. Irene and all of Bristol realised that the blitz they had so dreaded had come at last:

> The bombs simply rained down. Every time we came up out of the shelter to see what was happening, wine bottles came over from the warehouse nearby.

> The bombs dropped on the horses and sent the flesh over the wall. Each time we came out we were surrounded by parts of horses that had been blown up... wine, horses, you name it, it was coming at us. It was like almighty hell. You imagine a thunderstorm, you know, a real bad thunderstorm. This was just like six lots of thunder. It was terrible... you just can't imagine what it was like until you've been through it and got over it.

The heart of this dreadful storm of fire and explosions lay around the area of Bristol Bridge but severe damage wasn't restricted to the centre of the city. Residential districts were being hit too, including Bedminster, Knowle, St. George and Clifton. The city was not prepared or equipped or experienced to cope with the disaster that was now unfolding. Incendiaries kindled blaze after blaze in empty shops, offices, public buildings and homes. The bewildered, frightened full-time and part-time firemen and other emergency workers could only do their best in what rapidly became impossible circumstances.

Bill Morgan had been having tea with his mother and his future wife when his mother called him to the front door, exclaiming at 'the lovely lights in the sky' over Bristol. Bill realised just what those lovely lights meant and he hurried the two women down to the shelter. Then he donned his uniform and dashed off on his bicycle, pedalling furiously for the fire station at Brislington, about a mile and a half away:

> They had big Beresford pumps on the harbour and they were pumping gallons and gallons of water but the unpreparedness of it all showed then. The hose was an old canvas one and it was so full of holes that we had as much water coming out of the holes as we did from the nozzle. Somebody got hold of a load of tin baths and they were placed along the hose – you could hear the ping-pong-ping-pong as the water was coming out.

Bomb damage on what is now platform 3 at Temple Meads railway station: November 25, 1940

College Green, November 25, 1940. The leading furniture store, P E Gane, left in ruins

> When you're fighting a fire with HE bombs falling around you, there's so much
> damage that all you can really hope to do is to put the fire out quick enough to
> stop it becoming a target for the next load of bombers. There was no hope of
> saving buildings, not when there was exploding bombs as well. Anybody who
> said they weren't frightened, they weren't heroes, they were nuts. I felt terror-
> stricken, absolutely frightened to death, but you got used to it.

Bill Graves, serving in the ARP, was having just as dramatic a night in the Wine
Street/Castle Street area on the other side of the river. He had been sent to St. Peter's
Hospital, one of the finest remaining Tudor mansions in the country, to help rescue
monuments and archives from the already blazing buildings:

We were getting out chairs and bits and pieces when the ARP guy in charge pulled us back and suddenly we looked up and the lead on the roof of St. Peter's Church and St. Peter's Hospital had melted. It was starting to roll towards the river, like a silver stream. It was beautiful, there's no other expression for it, but it was dreadful. Then I was ordered to close off the bottom of Castle Street as the road was on fire.

After it had been closed off a green ambulance came down with a girl driving. She was only about 19, not much older than me. She asked where the Central Health Clinic was. They were still taking the casualties down there even though there was fire all around. This girl was as cool as a cucumber, and she had just come through Dante's Inferno.

It was an inferno that was by now raging unchecked. There were more than 70 large fires, many of which needed at least five pumps to fight them. But Bristol had only 224 appliances available. The city didn't have the manpower either. The fire brigade was under strength by 77 men with 995 full-time firemen in service. That was enough to man 96 appliances. The remaining appliances were being manned, wherever possible, by 897 part-time firemen. It was an equation with one inevitable, deadly outcome… Bristol became a city of flames.

William Hares, who lived in Merchant Street, Broadmead, kept a diary, describing the six major blitz attacks on Bristol, and how he did his bit:

My night off, and I take no notice of the early siren, but get ready to go to meet the wife and children in Old Market Street. Heavy gun fire! But I'm used to that, and it gives me no concern, but planes seem to be very low.

Suddenly the sky is lit with several flares. New experience, this. And I begin to get worried. Relieved to find wife and kiddies going into a nearby shelter. People are running like hell! There is a tension in the air like the prelude to a heavy thunderstorm. Little do we know what we'll have to face before the night's out. But I get my family home just as the first bombs start to fall.

The sky is now lit up with different coloured flares; the barrage is terrific, and the air is filled with the constant drone of Jerry planes, the scream of falling bombs and the thunder of their explosion. See my mates. 'We're in for a pasting tonight!' Both seem to think discretion the better part of valour, can't blame them, anyway. Got a very queer feeling myself; I'm terribly dry, and I don't quite know what to do, but decide I'll try and see it through.

Incendiaries start to fall in our own neighbourhood. Several fires in the City; more – and heavier – bombs dropping. Still windy, and the fires spread; new fires springing up now, adding a spectacular effect to the inferno of bombs and gunfire. Beginning to get used to it!

Incendiaries fall across the Barton. Two fall in our street: one on Jones's warehouse starts to smoke and burn. People trying to extinguish them with buckets of water. Terrific barrage: shell cap falls through a window, and I pick it up. Pick up another one that falls just where I am standing. Two early souvenirs!

German planes keep coming over. Don't feel so frightened now. But the centre of the city is one blazing mass; and the Jerries are plastering the fires with all they have. WHAT A NIGHT. Jones's warehouse enveloped in flames; firemen say they can do nothing. Everybody seems very calm, though none seems to know just what to do.

I go to the Warden's Post to see if anything can be done to stop the fires in our street. Little help forthcoming. The two lady telephonists – both perfectly calm – are working like the devil, trying to deal with the chaotic conditions.

More incendiaries, more bombs; more big fires. Hell is released on our city. Many soldiers are doing good work, but we've still no Fire Auxiliaries to deal with the local fires. Frontages begin to collapse! The din is tremendous. Glass and débris scattered everywhere. Flames spread to adjacent buildings. Soldiers shout for shovels to beat out the flames. It seems hopeless now, for the water supply has failed.

Mrs. S. is a heroine. She's making tea for everyone. The landlord of one pub is ready to joke, and tells customers that drinks are on the house, as he does not think there'll be a pub there in the morning! Horses, terror-stricken, are running wild in the streets.

Jones's fire is now dying out. But the Barton warehouse is a blazing beacon. Jerry's still letting us have it every minute. Think that I'm now accustomed to the bombs and the din, but when a fire bomb falls on Llewellins & James

A devastated Bridge Street somehow epitomises Bristolians' shattered morale

Salvage operations in Newfoundland Road

in the Green I'm really terrified. I'm caught in the middle of the street. I can't run; I can't duck; I can't shout. It's a ghastly sensation. I just want to gaze and see where the bomb falls. Like an express train with chains rattling, it comes hissing through the air, and falls with a dull thud. Four more come whistling down in Castle Street.

I recover from that shock. Nothing matters any more now, surely! C. and N. have come into the house to die together. 'God help us if anything should fall on our factory.' They're not showing up too well.

Jones's warehouse is now burnt out, but the adjoining buildings are burning furiously. Soldiers are trying to beat out the flames with coats and caps. It's hopeless. We've no fire pumps, although there is a river flowing beneath the road, and the hoses could be passed through the many manholes.

'Massed Raid on West Town. Another church hit by the midnight raider.' This photograph was passed by the censor, November 26, 1940 and published in the *Bristol Evening News*. This was Temple

More bombs fall on Broadmead. John Hall's starts to blaze. I pick up with a soldier who's got plenty of guts. People start salvaging from the apparently doomed shops and houses. It looks as if the whole block will be gutted. But there's still no sign of any firemen. WHERE THE HELL ARE THEY? Llewellins and James is now ablaze. What a night! And what a party!

My soldier pal gets a pump from somewhere and we try to put a fire out on the top of Price's roof. We smash in Hobson & Morris's door but cannot get to the fire from inside. Then a fireman lets us have a ladder, and up goes the soldier and I start to pump like hell. Now we get some assistance, although the buildings across the street are quite beyond control. The café is burning.

'The doll's house is safe', photographer Jim Facey wrote on the back of this picture

So is Lenton's, now set alight by the flying sparks carried by the rising wind. J. Hall's now a raging mass. Castle Green is too, and Llewellins & James's seems to be white hot. Bombs and more bombs! Barton warehouses are nearly burnt out; but the fire is now raging on the other side of the street. A truly majestic sight – oddly enough – from our roof.

Don't seem to mind bombs now. Suppose I have got used to them, or else it's because I've seen other people ignore them. Funny how you can get used to anything if you have to.

Auxiliary pumps are now on the job. It's a crew from outside, and they don't know where the hydrants or manholes are. Eventually they are told of manholes, but have trouble with the covers and it seems hours before they manage to prise them open. Now the pumps are going and the firemen get busy, it sort of gives you a comforting feeling. Takes your mind off Jerries and bombs!

What a night. Don't think it possible to survive the raid, although the fires that surround us are a sight no one could ever forget. Jerry seems to be easing off. Planes not coming in so fast, nor does the barrage seem so continuous. No idea of the time. My eyes are one streaming mess, and I can hardly see.

Find the street strewn with cobble stones. Soldier says one just missed him and that he'd better move his car from the blaze. That was the last I saw of him. He was a great lad.

Tell my wife it will probably go on until 2.00 a.m. Jerry now seems to have spent his force. He's only coming over occasionally, but what a beacon he has lit aided by the wind! Like a snowstorm; only this 'snow' is red and black.

Firemen doing good work and some of the fires are burning themselves out. Blitz seems to have finished. Suppose Jerry's used up all his planes and bombs. Only sounds now are the pumps, the crackling of the flames, and the falling masonry.

GLORY BE! IT'S THE ALL CLEAR. What a marvellous sound, and what a reprieve from hell. I never expected to hear it again, and I really can't believe I'm hearing it now. The first blitz is ended… but the fires rage on.

Teenager Norman Allan went to meet his friends at Eastville Park:

Jerry was over before the sirens went. We were all sat around and we could hear them coming towards us as it gradually got louder and louder. Then they started dropping bombs. My brother shouted at us all to get down. They all got down bar myself – I was a bit late. I felt a thud in my chest and a burning sensation. I remember lying there, my brother was with me and my friends left to go to the air-raid shelter.

Two girls walked towards us, two ATS girls who asked my brother if there was anything they could do. One of them put her haversack under my head as a pillow. They stayed with us. God knows how long I stayed there. Eventually an auxiliary ambulance came collecting the injured, driven by two girls. They had to go up roads that were burning, the bombing was still going on. The flames were leaping up and they had to stop, turn round and go back. They were marvellous. Eventually we ended up at the Bristol General Hospital. I was still conscious. I remember being taken to a room and my clothes being cut off me. Then I passed out.

Mae Rae was a bus conductor.

I was conducting on the night of the terrible November raid, on the Sunday. We were going into town from Brislington and when the siren went we dropped the passengers at the nearest shelter, that was the regulation. The driver had to take the bus back to the depot while I went to Old Market Street to pay in the money. I was in the underground canteen when the bombs started, and the police brought children in from the Empire Theatre nearby, and we

The indomitable British spirit: a chef from Jones's department store sets up an impromptu kitchen in the ruins of St Mary-le-Port Street

played tunes to them on comb and paper. When we came out, we walked up West Street and I could see people in doorways. I thought they had fainted and wanted to help, but in fact they were dead from the blast.

Across the city centre at the Colston Hall, Gladys Locke and her husband were at last allowed to leave. The building was unscathed and she was anxious to hurry off to her mother's home in Brislington as quickly as possible.

> The walk through the city was, well, I don't think anybody could describe it. There were buildings falling down, there were rescue operations going on with all the people buried, there was water gushing in the streets, there were gas mains going. You had to pick your way through where you could get through. But there were fires and the smell of gas and people shouting and screaming. And crowds of people huddled about with blankets over them and ambulances running here, there and everywhere. It was terrible.

Gladys and her husband struggled through the rubble-littered streets and made the long, weary trudge to her mother's home to find her sheltering in the coal house, terrified but unhurt.

Damage to trunk water mains inevitably caused a shortage of water, and 77 outside brigades were asked for help, but mostly they arrived too late. Bad supervision and lack of experience, shortage of men and working appliances meant that the heart of the city burned far more fiercely than it need have done. Firemen found they also had to do rescue work wherever the rescue services were unable to get through.

In fact, post-mortems on the November 24 raid suggest, with hindsight, that more buildings were lost than need have been: a report said that 'a great many of the ancient city churches could have been saved if their congregations had organised fire-watching'; the Dutch House was pulled down by the army two days after the raid, despite an assessment that only the top floors were badly damaged on one side, and that the much loved landmark could have been restored. Nobody had the time to organise a protest and insist on its conservation.

This was the most serious raid that Bristol had yet experienced. The bomber crews were briefed to focus their attention on the harbour and industrial plant on both sides of the City Docks, with the intention of eliminating Bristol as an important port sup-

Picking through the remains of St Clement's Church, Newfoundland Road

plying much of the Midlands and south of England. Although poor weather over the Continent meant that the attack was of shorter duration than intended, lasting only four hours, for the Germans it was a very successful night with 156.25 tonnes of high explosives, 4.75 tonnes of oil bombs and 12,500 incendiaries dropped on target for the loss of just two aircraft.

The situation was probably made worse because the Fire Guard organisation had yet to be formed, and on a Sunday evening the city centre was deserted with the majority of the commercial premises securely locked. Additionally, at this period, most buildings lacked any easy access to their vulnerable roof areas, where a single incendiary bomb could start a fire almost invisible to observers on the ground. In this manner a number of tall buildings, such as churches, were burnt down and by midnight the city was blazing furiously, the glow in the sky being visible up to 60 miles away.

When dawn broke, on November 25, it was a dismal scene. Smoke still rose from the débris, there were flickers of flame from remaining fires, and the air was heavy with the choking bitter smell of scorched timber and masonry. The streets were filthy with blackened water from the night's fire fighting efforts and glass lay everywhere.

People wandered about, numbed by the sight of so many familiar landmarks reduced to smoking piles of rubble. More than 10,000 homes had been damaged, factories had been hit, churches destroyed. Some of the city's finest architectural heritage had vanished in the night or been left in ruins.

The Dutch House was a skeleton, St. Peter's Church and St. Peter's Hospital were damaged beyond repair. With them had gone Bristol's most popular shopping centre, in the busy streets around Wine Street and Castle Street. This was where shoppers used to gather in their thousands, and now it was a city of the dead.

It took some days before the dead could be counted. The final tally was 207 killed, 187 seriously injured, and another 703 slightly injured. The death toll included eight firemen, 22 ARP wardens, two ARP messengers and two ambulance drivers. Almost 1,400 had been made homeless and water, gas and electricity supplies had been badly disrupted.

The siege of Bristol had truly begun.

Victim: one of thousands of wartime pictures taken by *Evening Post* photographer Jim Facey

A DIFFICULT CHRISTMAS

When the German bombers came over in force on the night of December 2-3 in the second big blitz on the city, Bristolians knew what to expect.

Over four hours, 121 aircraft dropped 120 tonnes of high explosives, a tonne of oil bombs and 22,000 incendiaries. The damage was more widespread, with the main bombing concentrated on a line running through Redfield, St. Paul's, Cotham and Redland. The Luftwaffe lost only one plane, which crashed on take-off. Once again there were complaints about Bristol's inadequate land and air defences.

From the diary of William Hares:

> Siren goes. N. and A. have not arrived yet. I'm listening to the News, but the gun-fire is very heavy. Look out and see flares dropping over Clifton way. Tell Mr. C. they've started their nonsense again.

> My other two mates have left us in the lurch again. Only two of us to look after three buildings. Have to make wife take shelter. Tell her we're in for another pasting.

> Plenty of planes in the sky. Intermittent gun-fire. Seems as if Avonmouth is getting it.

> Tell a young lady to take cover. Give same warning to a young man and his girlfriend, who seems very frightened, but who says that she has only to die once. Pick up with a deaf fellow, and ask him to lend me a hand. He's quite willing, and shows no fear. He's been to sea and has been torpedoed. Just the right man in a pinch!

> Bombs dropping nearer now. Have to lay down several times. Somehow, though, it's not like the first night. I suppose the thought of getting through one blitz makes it an odds-on chance of seeing this lot over. Big blaze in middle of town, and Jerries seem to be concentrating on that.

> Bombs whistling down. Funny to see the deaf man fall down when I do, like a one-man act. There's a very close one!! We're covered with blue sparks. Everything seems to rock.

Damage to E S & A Robinson's premises, December 1940

The wife's all right, although she cannot get the children to sleep. The people in the house are now quite all right. The wife shows them how to keep their chins up.

Barrage intermittent. Not so continuous as the first blitz. Policeman says our planes are up. Then we get some excitement in our sector. Incendiaries fall across the Friar's roof, and the beams start to blaze. I cycle round to the Warden's Post to report it.

Return to find Mr. T., the caretaker, and a policeman silhouetted against the red glow of a big fire across Newfoundland Street, taking no notice of the stuff that is falling. Then, with a swish, another string of fire bombs comes sailing down across the road. We think they have missed us, and go across the road to see where they have fallen.

Glory be! Our own building's ablaze. I didn't know what to think for the moment. The fire seemed to be out of control in a few minutes. I shouted to 'Deaffy' to follow me, and we rush up the stairs. Fire has caught the beams and there is the sound of hissing. 'Deaffy' starts to put out the flames on the second floor with his foot and cap. I rush to the top floor and let the bomb there have it with a bucketful of water. The worst thing I could have done, for the whole thing went up in a sheet of white flame. Fire seemed to spread all around me. I got panicky, and started to back away. Threw sand on to the fire, and was surprised to see the flames die down.

'Deaffy' had now stamped and almost put out the fire on the second floor; we got to work with stirrup pump, and in no time it seemed that the job was finished. So I stuck out my chest.

The fires tonight seem to have been got under control much quicker than I thought they would. Practice must make perfect. Harris's across the road starts to burn. Flames coming from glass fanlight. Looks like a big fire. Dash round to the Warden's Post, but a messenger is already on the way. On returning, a Jerry plane comes in low and lets go his load of hate. It falls quite near, and my bike seems to be sucked across the road. Another explosion. Phew! That was a close 'un.

At the ready: an ARP warden in a Bristol suburb

Again we are between two fires, because the Dockland Settlement buildings beyond are blazing. But, despite tonight's fires, there is not the same excitement as there was on the first night's blitz. Must be getting blasé.

Things are now easing off and we now wait for the All Clear. Jerry has not had it all his own way tonight, and I don't think he has done so much damage – considering the length of the raid – as he did the first time.

This is a contemporary report on how a woman ARP warden spent the night shift of December 2-3.

She had been on duty since 10.00 p.m. when the night raid began. She first assisted a woman who was buried up to her neck, gave her a cup of tea and stood by for half an hour helping in the rescue work. Unfortunately that woman she had helped subsequently died. The woman warden then rescued a small boy and handed him to the First Aid party. Continuing her search for victims, she found a foot protruding from the rubble. After removing the débris, the headless body of a man was found. Then, on hearing that a baby was missing, she searched the area, found the child and restored it to the

Part of Bristol's ground defences

mother. Afterwards she came upon a woman whose husband had been killed and whose four children were missing. She comforted the woman and found out where her children were. Numerous dead bodies were collected and covered up by her during her duties, while all the time the bombs were falling. She was instructed at 8.30 a.m. the following morning to leave her duty and obtain some rest, but she refused and carried on for some hours more.

That raid cost 156 lives with another 149 people seriously injured. Services were very badly disrupted. Once again the cold weather made life in the many damaged homes that much more wretched.

The Luftwaffe came back in force on the night of December 6, in a third blitz which

King George VI visits blitzed Bristol, December 1940. The Lord Mayor is Alderman T H Underdown

killed 100, injured 188, and caused another crack in morale. A great deal of damage was caused by fires in St. Philip's Marsh, Temple Meads, the city centre and Cotham, as William Hares reported:

> Warning. All on duty, be ready for anything. Look forward to some action. Gun-fire heavy. Plenty of planes about. Some flares dropped but it seems the Jerries are after something else tonight.

> Then fire watcher calls out to us to observe a plane in the searchlights. Planes are very low tonight. Some damned good pilots, I should think. We are all waiting for something to happen.

> More planes, swarms of them, although they all seem to be passing over the town, and leaving us alone. Everyone appears to be on tip-toe tonight. Now a Jerry plane makes a smoke sign. Think at first it has been hit by the Ack-Ack, but it passes out of sight.

The City Docks were a prime target: the Granary, Prince's Wharf, January 4, 1941

Reported to be the biggest bomb dropped on Britain during the war.
Nicknamed Satan, the device landed in Beckington Road, Knowle on January 3, 1941

More flares. Still no action. Then a few incendiaries fall. One near the 'Mail Coach', and a War Reserve Constable takes a flying kick at it. It's soon put out. Then comes the heavy stuff. There is a glow in the sky from the docks, and over Temple Meads and Redcliffe Way fires start to burn furiously. We wait for more incendiaries, though there seems little doing in our particular neighbourhood.

City Mill catches fire, but firemen are soon on the job. It's blazing fiercely. Firemen told of manholes in the street, and they get to work quickly, and soon have the pumps going. Jerry is still coming over, but there seem to be several minute intervals between the planes.

Wife gets firemen some tea, but they are too busy to drink it. A big and heavy direct hit on the little 'Gem' cinema is scored. Luckily the fire-watcher had moved away in time. Mr. B. says it lifted him off the floor.

Tonight it seems that most of the fires are quickly got under control, and everybody carried on just as a matter of fact. If a big 'un falls near, they joke about it, and people are out in the streets watching the fire-fighters.

City Mill now well under control, but there's a big fire in Bridge Street.

Early All Clear. Another blitz has been borne and survived!

After that raid 1940 came to a close without any more major attacks, but the continual air raid warnings as the bombers made their way to other targets further inland meant sleepless nights, and the weather grew colder in a city of broken windows, patched roofs, damaged buildings and disrupted public services.

On the evening of Friday, January 3, 1941, people heard the hated drone of enemy bombers heading towards Bristol once again. It was the start of what developed into one of the longest air raids experienced anywhere at this stage of the war. The sirens sounded at 6.21 p.m. and, as the attack began, the city's heavy anti-aircraft artillery went into action. Then, after just 10 minutes, the sound of the Bristol guns died away. Bristolians listening from their shelters couldn't understand what had gone wrong and why bombs were falling without answering fire from our guns. They might have been reassured if they had known the answer. Air Intelligence had learnt several hours before that Bristol was to be the target of another blitz, and this time the RAF wanted to give its night fighters a chance to beat the bombers. So, as the first enemy aircraft approached, night-flying Hurricanes were scrambled and all anti-aircraft artillery ordered to shut down to give the Hurricanes a free rein to attack the Germans. As things turned out, the fighters did nothing to stem the assault during their allotted hour over Bristol while the silent guns angered and frightened the people shivering in whatever shelters they could find on that sub-zero night. Hopes that this might be a short raid were raised when an All Clear sounded at 8.59 p.m.

Moreen Sellers was one of many thousands who sighed with relief when she heard that All Clear. She had been sheltering under the stairs of her Bedminster home with her brother, mother and grandmother. Her father, who worked for the tramways company, was away at work. The next day was to be her brother's ninth birthday. As the All Clear died away, her mother left their cupboard refuge to make some tea while her grandmother went to sit by the fire to warm herself against the cold. She took the children's socks with her and hung them in front of the fire. Within a couple of minutes, the air raid sirens were howling again.

The German bombers hadn't gone away, they were still over Bristol. My brother and I put on the warm socks and went back into the cupboard. We had beds there under the stairs. Mother was making tea in the scullery and the lights went out. Mother dropped everything and dived under the dining room table. It was all quiet. It seemed such a long time that I was waiting for something to happen and suddenly I could hear this sort of soft crackle in the roof and it grew louder and louder and then it all came down on us. All the dust and the smell of the smoke around us and my grandmother shouting 'Oh help, oh God help me.' The stairs took the weight of a lot of it, the roof and the furniture and things that were upstairs. Then everything was all quiet and it was all dusty and horrible. It seemed an eternity. My brother and I had our heads sort of stuck and we couldn't move. It wasn't hurting but we couldn't move and then, after a long, long time we heard some men saying 'Don't worry, we'll get you out, don't panic.'

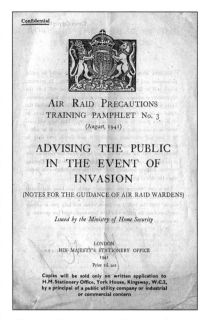

This confidential pamphlet issued to Air Raid Wardens explains what to do in an invasion, amongst other things how to immobilise a car or bicycle

They were moving things and digging and pushing things away and they got my brother and me out and took us to the air raid shelter at E.S. and A. Robinson, quite near. I didn't know what had happened to my mother; then I heard she had been taken away with my grandmother in a lorry with tarpaulin over the top. No one spoke to us in the shelter. They should have said hullo, like you speak to children, but I suppose they were all concerned with their own homes. They knew we'd been bombed and they lived near us, so I suppose they got frightened thinking what they'd find when they got out.

The All Clear went. My brother started crying. He said, 'What are we going to do?' and I said 'Don't worry about it, we'll take you down to Auntie Winn's and Uncle Bob's', my mother's brother. We began walking, in the middle of the road. My father always said that if you've got to go out after an air raid, then walk in the middle of the road because you'll be away from falling slates and things from roofs and incendiary bombs in shop doorways or gardens. My brother kept saying,'Who's going to look after us?' and I told him not to worry, that I was his big sister. And I was only a year and 11 months older than him. It was just lucky, my uncle came towards us and asked what we were doing. So of course I broke down and cried and told him that Gran and Mum had been taken away and I didn't know where. He took us in and said he'd find Mummy and Grandma when it was light.

Meanwhile Moreen's father, who had spent a busy night helping to drive as many buses as possible out of Bristol to the safety of the countryside so that the city would have public transport once the blitz was over, had arrived home to find his house destroyed and his family missing.

He had thought we were all dead underneath all that rubble. He walked into my aunt's house and saw us and we ran into his arms and we all cried together; we just cried and cried and cried. My two uncles went all around Bristol to all the hospitals and found my mother but my grandmother had died.

Moreen's mother survived. Her vision was badly affected by the shock and blast of the direct hit and her eyes remained bandaged for many weeks. Gradually her eyesight recovered but the family's nerves were gone, shattered by their ordeal. Before long they found refuge in Chewton Mendip, outside Bristol and away from the bombing.

The final, true All Clear sounded at 6.21 a.m., exactly 12 hours after the initial warning. The raid had been savage, as Bristol discovered in the light of dawn. More than 180 aircraft had been sent to pound Bristol and only 14 failed to reach the target. To make matters worse for the emergency services trying to cope with the disaster, the severe cold badly hampered fire-fighting, with water rapidly freezing in the open air. The centre of Bristol, Bedminster, Knowle and Clifton all suffered hits. About 2,500 houses were damaged and 149 people were killed, 133 seriously injured and more than 200 slightly hurt.

Gerald Smith and his brothers and sisters were handed food and hot drinks by the Salvation Army when they emerged from the shelter of the Portway tunnel that bleak January morning.

Regent Street, Clifton

Their walk home through the streets of a blitzed Bristol was a terrible experience for Gerald and so many other children who witnessed the results of a protracted air raid:

> When we got to the main street near our home, all the houses were caved in on the street. There were hose pipes, dogs barking, sirens going, burglar alarms sounding, an absolute cacophony of war. When we got to what we thought was our street, there were many corpses laid on the corner and the pavement was sloping up to the houses. I remember blood was running from the bodies into the main road and this went on down the road, as if somebody was tipping buckets of red paint. We saw people walking along with parts of torsos, matching them with shoes or coats, piecing them together, which was very distressing. We talked about it among ourselves that first day. When we

Bristol Evening Post, January 17 1941.

BRISTOL
EVENING POST

"Fall in, the Fire-Bomb Fighters"—HERBERT MORRISON.

No. 2,718 | Phone No.: Bristol 20080 | **FRIDAY, JANUARY 17, 1941.** | ONE PENNY

ATTACK ON BRISTOL
LASTS 10 HOURS

Fire Parties Respond Magnificently to The Challenge, and Quickly 'Put Paid' to Incendiaries

PATIENTS HELP AT A HOSPITAL

CIVILIAN fire parties responded magnificently last night to the latest challenge flung down by German raiders when a 10-hour attack—from just after dusk to dawn—was launched against Bristol.

NAZI PLANES ATTACKED MALTA

NAVY READY FOR DIVE BOMBERS

Stefani Agency, Rome, declares that it was German bombers which made Wednesday's intense air attacks on Malta.

Incendiaries were pounced on the moment they had fallen, and this display of high courage was of the greatest assistance to and the admiration of the fire brigades.

Two churches were destroyed, a hospital was damaged by fire, and, when some

ON THE "NAIL"

THE BRISTOL "NAILS," once used by merchants in lieu of tables, are again being utilised by grain merchants. The blacked-out glass roof inside the Exchange, Corn Street, does not allow sufficient daylight to judge the quality of the grain. This familiar Thursday morning scene of business being conducted on one of the famous brass pillars.

GREEKS CAPTURE PATROL

Little Remains Big Nazi Po

Bombers of the R.A.F. another concentrated on the naval ba Wilhelmshaven last u Reports so far receive that this operation w highly successful.

IT was more than a fo attack to the p bombing, and was as c planned and as system carried out as the one d by a pilot as more like " than bombing."

Once again the raid was against the very definite o in the port, which in many may be described as repres combination of Portsmou Plymouth.

Last night the strenuou that the Nazis were ma restore order out of the created by our bombers on day were further hampere fresh arrivals, who raine more bombs.

TERRIFIC BARRAG

As the result of the t the war industrial side helmshaven may hav reduced to a state of wre The British pilots had to gauntlet of a terrific barr greater than any in any of in Germany, for Wilhelm

Evening Post January 17, 1941. Upbeat report of heroism in the face of savage attack on the city

went to school, we said, 'What have you seen?' In the end, we became so hardened we could talk about our daily scan of what we'd seen and be competitive about it and, of course, things did get out of proportion.

As with every raid, stories came out of the amazing courage and endurance of ordinary people. Mr. H. Davies was later to recall:

In November 1940, I was in Southmead Hospital when incendiaries dropped all round. Then the bombs came, and we just had to get under our beds. Then I went to the General Hospital on January 3, 1941, to have an anaesthetic examination. While I was unconscious the sirens sounded, and when I came round I was being carried to the basement. I shall never forget that night. Children were crying and women moaning, but Matron, doctors and nurses were very brave, bringing round hot drinks for the patients. Opposite me was a man sitting up on a stretcher; he had eight nurses around him, and had them all singing: 'I've got sixpence, jolly, jolly sixpence.' All this time the roof was on fire and bombs were falling.

Then the order came through to move all patients to the BRI. I shall never forget that journey! When we arrived we were taken right to the top of the building; as one patient said, they must have thought we were the suicide squad! Jerry was still letting them fall, and every time we heard a bomb we had to dive under the bed. The next day we were all sent home, and I arrived in just an operating shirt and a pair of bedsocks. The same night incendiaries fell in our district – we had 21 fires in roofs and bedrooms in our street alone, and I went out to lend a hand. Next day I went for my clothes to the GH., only to find that someone had lifted £5.10s. out of my pocket, leaving me a key and a shilling. I still have this as a keepsake.

Mrs. Fane, of Ashton Vale:

My sister was a warden all through the blitzes. On January 3, 1941, an incendiary fell through the roof of a house near which my sister was standing. She raced across to the house and found the inmates playing a game. 'There's an incendiary upstairs,' she shouted. They at once started to remove the furniture, but my sister said 'Leave all that. It's upstairs,' and she ran up to the room where it was. It had gone clean through the bed, and was burning its way through the floor.

She could find no sand, water, or earth, so ran outside and started scratching up some earth from the frozen ground with her finger nails. Then she crawled under the bed and was just going to throw the earth on the bomb when 'Swish!' – a bucket of water landed right in her face. A man had heard cries for water, and filled a bucket; knowing the bomb was under the bed he rushed up stairs and flung the icy water on it without realising that my sister was there. The water froze on her face and legs!

Shortly after the All Clear we heard that our old home in Bedminster was partially demolished. A bomb had fallen in my aunt's garden and swept half the street away. My sister and I, without having any rest, went at once to Stafford Street, Mill Lane, there to find chaos. We worked all the Saturday until nearly tea-time, toiling with a salvage party, to get away as much as we could from what was once our home.

Bristol was singled out for one more major attack that month. On the night of January 16, 126 Luftwaffe bombers flew over Avonmouth and Bristol in a nine-hour raid, the target being the Avonmouth and Bristol Docks, and Parnall Aircraft at Yate. There was considerable damage, though only 18 people were killed. The following day was the only one of the entire war when the docks were prevented from working normally.

Another diarist (and member of the Mass Observation team), V.A. Maund, noted the results of this raid.

> Thurs., Jan 16: Sirens went at 8.25 p.m. and the 'All clear' at 5.45 this morning. Of course, no sleep all night, during the ten-hour raid. Rang up M. at Clifton, to learn their house had suffered severe damage, the roof being torn off, and a mantelpiece blown out. M., who was ill, in bed, had to leave her bed owing to the heavy bombardment. After the raid, a large brick was found on the pillow of her bed. It would almost certainly have killed her had she remained in bed.

> Sat., Jan 18: A blitz on Swansea during the night. It started on Bristol, but petered out owing to the A.A. gun barrage, which forced the enemy to cross the Bristol Channel. Deep snow on the ground this morning.

> Tues., Jan. 21: Visited M. at Clifton. She is still in bed, ill, but downstairs. Took her some eggs and onions. All their roof is gone, and their top-floor ceiling is only tarpaulin. A bomb made a 30-feet-deep crater in their front garden, and they were unable to get out of their house until dug out by the ARP men. The gas main shot up a flame higher than the house, thus scaring everyone, as, in the darkness, it made them an easy target for the enemy 'upstairs'.

January 1941 was probably the lowest point during Bristol's siege. For it was one of the grimmest winters on record, and Bristolians had lost confidence in the city shelters. Many of them had begun to desert the city at night and others sought out unofficial shelters in caves and tunnels and mines. Was the city losing its nerve?

MORALE

Bristol had become accustomed to dozens of small raids, in the run up to the November 24-25 blitz of 1940; but after that every alert could signal a major bombardment. So the major concern of the authorities, locally and nationally, was how the citizens would react. Would law and order be maintained? Would people be able to cope with constant fear, stress, damaged homes, shortages, power cuts, would they lose their nerve and flee the city?

What those in charge were worried about was that indefinable thing, morale, that feeling of physical and psychological readiness for whatever happened, the ability to carry on without becoming frightened, pessimistic or defeatist.

So building morale became all important, and in Bristol it was constantly being measured. It is probably just as well that Bristol didn't know about a secret report on its morale during the Blitz. For while Bristolians thought they were coping with the Blitz as well as any other city, the secret report said that Bristolians were more depressed, more nervy, and more defeatist than the people of Coventry, Plymouth and Southampton.

Morale, and the fostering of it, was the keynote of the propaganda war on the home front in the Second World War. But how do you measure it?

Mass Observation, started in 1937 as a grass roots social survey organisation, had its fingers on the pulse of the nation. It selected volunteers to keep diaries, and go around listening for comments on selected topics: they would eavesdrop on conversations in pubs and shops and cinemas, and record reactions. Several Mass Observers were keeping their eyes and ears open in Bristol during the Blitz.

But Mass Observation also had a special investigation team which went round blitzed cities, after the raids, to assess morale and public attitudes, and their report on Bristol caused a secret furore. For the team, which visited Bristol three times at intervals between December 19, 1940, and April 2, 1941, came to the conclusion that Bristol was suffering from poor morale and unimaginative leadership.

It was this latter charge which caused the secret outrage, for the independent MO report was never intended for publication, and so did not mince words. It was prepared

Which one are you? Sisters being evacuated at Temple Meads railway station

regardless of official accounts, departmental feelings, or patriotic propaganda.

The few civic leaders and Cabinet Ministers who did see it complained to Herbert Morrison, who, after reading it, demanded the withdrawal of all copies. The local dignitaries complained that it was the work of 'a few intellectuals with nothing better to do'.

High-ranking officials described it as an extraordinary mixture of fact, fiction and dangerous mischief, and Morrison resented the circulation of what he felt was 'ill-founded criticism without any attempt to check accuracy'. So the document remained secret, and did not become available until the mid-1970s.

The report said that Bristolians were coping far less well with the raids than people in other parts of the country. The population was less cheerful: they did not joke about the raids, they gathered morbidly for weeks around the bomb sites, they listened regularly to the broadcasts by Lord Haw-Haw from Germany, indulged in defeatist talk, and spread rumours. 'We found nothing like the dislocation and multiple personal discomforts which still dominate private and domestic life in Southampton or Coventry,' said the investigators, who found a fortnight after the November 24 raid that telephones were working, hot food was being supplied to the homeless, and that bomb damage was less than in Coventry or Southampton.

> Despite all this, there is more depression in Bristol than in any other area studied in recent months. There is a quite open defeatism, especially among the young workers, though the Lord Mayor and others appear to have a somewhat exaggerated idea of its potentialities. There is also much more wishful thinking about the war soon being over than in other areas, in itself probably an indication of depression.

> … The main grumble is about the shelters. There is a violent minority dissatisfaction with Bristol shelters and this is certainly often spontaneous, non-political, and actually justified.

> Investigators with a wide comparison of experience with town shelter facilities consider those in Bristol to be strikingly inferior and inadequate in many parts of the town.

The local Mass Observers collected some damning quotes from Bristolians, showing their defeatism: 'I can't see how we're going to win this war.' 'Why don't we call an

Awaiting the unknown: Bristol children *en route* to the West Country

armistice?' 'Of course we're losing, we're only one little country.' They reported that 12 days after the November 24 raid people were still gazing at the wrecked buildings and saying gloomily: 'It'll never be the same again.'

But there was another, positive side to Bristol's reaction to that first big raid. It came from comradeship in disaster, a shared sense of loss, a new team spirit. Home Intelligence, which was keeping a close watch on civilian reaction to blitz raids, took note of all the grumbles but concluded that Bristol's morale was good and that the city had takes the blow on the chin. There was grim determination in this moment of adversity.

The citizens took the blow almost lightheartedly at first. Co-operation and

Nurses survey the wreckage at Bristol Homeopathic Hospital

practical good neighbourliness limited dislocation to a great extent. But by November 28, when people were becoming tired from their exertions, when the lack of water here of gas there and transport difficulties nearly everywhere became increasingly irksome, this mood became more serious. The fact remains that the people of the West Country are stout hearted and without thought of surrender.

Whenever it was possible, the majority of the citizens went about their business as usual. The rhythm of everyday existence was maintained; otherwise the life of the city would have been brought to a standstill. Whatever might have occurred on the previous night, the baker still went on his rounds in the morning, and the milkman and the postman came, though sometimes late. Shops and banks were open; buses ran and thousands of housewives stood for hours in ever lengthening queues. Typists and shop

Life must go on: a mobile shop comes to Bedminster

assistants turned up punctually even though the way to work lay through débris-encumbered streets. Factory workers in their thousands clocked in and even the humble charwoman with her scrubbing brush was there, sometimes a little before her time in order to help in clearing up the mess.

The spirit of Bristolians under siege came out best in their cheeky slogans. Bombed-out shops would put up notices saying 'More Open Than Shut'. A ruined wall would have 'Stick No Bills' on it. A bakery said: 'Hitler has paid us a visit, why don't you?' One barber's shop thought of: 'We've had a close shave' and a tailor: 'Hitler suits nobody, I suit everybody.' 'No Window Cleaners Wanted' went up on shops with their windows missing, and a lorry had a sign chalked on its side: 'If you can't be cheerful, shut up!'

Almondsbury cottagers survey their few salvaged possessions after a raid.
As with many photographs in this book, the censor banned publication

A scene repeated time and again throughout the city

Extremely popular in Bristol was this sample of moral uplift from Moral Re-Armament, printed on 50,000 give-away leaflets:

Morale – How You Can Play Your Part

Forget yourself in helping your neighbours – this casts out your own fears and worries.

Keep the moral standards of the nation high – make a break with all personal indulgences, selfishness and private wars which undermine morale and national unity.

Be a rumour stopper – any patriot shoots rumour dead on sight.

The secret of steadiness and inner strength is to listen to God and do what He says.

Forearm yourself by listening to God first thing every morning – this provides a clear plan for each day.

A British General who has fought through two wars said this: 'To listen to God and obey Him is the highest form of national service.'

One cause of low morale was the censorship of the press by the Ministry of Information. After the November 24-25 raid, the *Evening Post* on the Monday carried seven terse paragraphs about the horrors of the night before. 'It was stated that the casualties were comparatively few.' Another brisk morale-boosting line said that 'the men of the fire and ARP services performed stupendous labours in bringing the flames under control.' The *Evening Post*'s then headquarters were in Silver Street, Broadmead, in the heart of the inferno.

The one thing that everyone is hungry for during a war is information. And that was just what the Ministry of Information, a truly Orwellian title, wanted to suppress. The Ministry was concerned with controlling and managing information rather than with spreading it.

Disgruntled Bristolians would see their city shattered by a raid, and then read a report in the *Evening World* which gave no details of where the raid took place, what was bombed, how many died, or which factories, businesses and streets were hit.

They were simply not allowed to. The Ministry of Information issued a set statement which the papers and radio could publish, and then a few days later, when the Air Ministry was satisfied that the Germans had indeed intended to bomb Bristol, the fact was released that the West town in question was Bristol.

Bristol can take it!
'Our reply to this: the gift of a Spitfire'

Every newspaper editor was given documents known as the Defence Notices, listing subjects on which nothing could be published. They received a stream of notices and memos (one editor said he had 5,000 of them) adding to the list of banned topics. Weather forecasts were banned, for example; no mention of power stations or factories was allowed; and the MOI even suggested the editorial handling of certain topics. In theory, comment was free, and the national press was indeed critical of the management of the war, but provincial editors played the game, and consulted the MOI on anything they thought might be controversial.

Censorship was so strict that even births, marriages and deaths columns were vetted to see if there was any mention of the locations or movements of servicemen or ships. (No names of ships were ever mentioned: the censors even struck out references to *HMS Pinafore*!)

No readers' letters that might be critical of local authorities or the government were ever published, and even advertisements which indicated that a shop had moved premises because of the bombing were ruled out; Moss Bros in Bristol got into trouble in December 1940 for an advertisement which gave an indication of the extent of their damage, and their location.

With the best of motives, the public was left in the dark. After a heavy raid, Bristolians would naturally be anxious about relatives in another part of the city – but the papers could give no details of which streets had been bombed. Information was posted only in the streets.

ME109s on the Tramway Centre: morbid curiosity

Photographs were equally censored: all that were taken had to be submitted to the censor, who stamped them either 'Passed for publication' or 'Not to be published'.

Photographs of demolished factories, shops, historic buildings, churches or hospitals were not published, not only because they could show the enemy that their bombing had been effective, but because they might lower the morale of the citizens who lived in the area. No pictures of raging fires, rescues, or of bodies, were used, nor photographs showing people distressed and frightened.

Only morale-boosting pictures, of victims carrying on regardless despite the rubble, of cheerful people salvaging furniture from their homes, of cheery notices outside bomb-blasted shops were allowed. Queues were not photographed, nor were shelters, crying children, or homeless animals. No pictures of the trekkers who left the city nightly were ever seen.

Since the citizens of Bristol knew the reality of the Blitz, this censorship caused great resentment. They felt they were not trusted, and that the civil authorities were trying to pull the wool over their eyes, as well as the enemy's.

Since it was impossible to complain via the newspapers without being labelled a Communist or a subversive, people took to writing letters of protest to their local councillors, to the Lord Mayor, to their MPs, to members of the Cabinet and to the Royal family. Deprived of hard information, people relied on rumours. The first of hundreds of rumours came in 1939, with a false tale of shortages of tea and coffee that resulted in huge queues outside Carwardines.

Rumours in Bristol during the Blitz ranged from the hopeful to the ridiculous: it was said that some of the bombs dropped were filled only with sawdust, that the Germans bombed Arnos Vale cemetery because they thought the

gravestones were lines of army tents, and that contaminated food was being sold from warehouses that were bombed and open to the weather.

After the Baedeker raid on Bath, it was believed that bodies were laid out in the fields nearby because the mortuaries were full. The 'bodies' were in fact sleeping people who had taken to the countryside for safety. It was also believed in Bristol that the citizens of Bath were starving, and that they would all be evacuated.

Another persistent rumour was that a new and virulent strain of flu, caused by the raids, had arrived in the city. The Emergency Committee blamed milk and bread roundsmen for spreading the bad news.

Rumour-spreading was such a regular sport in Bristol that the local MOI tried to run as Anti-Rumour Campaign, getting people to take a pledge not to spread gossip, and to report all rumour-mongers to the police. An advertisement in the local press pro-

A Heinkel III falls to the fire of an RAF fighter

Richard Murdoch and Arthur Askey in 'Band Wagon', broadcast from a Clifton parish hall early in the war

claimed 'Rumour-Mongers Are Bad Citizens', but the grapevine went on regardless.

Some of the rumours did have a basis in fact: the stories of petrol and coal shortages in the winter of 1941 were indeed true. Sir Hugh Elles, the Regional Controller, had to demand immediate action from the Minister for Home Security, Herbert Morrison, when coal stocks were down to one week's supply. He wrote in a secret report of an 'impending calamity': 'Nothing short of another air attack would depress public morale as much as empty grates.'

It was simply the lack of information that drove people wild: it led them, in Bristol particularly as Mass Observers noted, to listen regularly to the Lord Haw-Haw pro-German propaganda broadcasts. 'They gave the same information as the BBC, but two days sooner,' was the justification one observer overheard.

Another odd by-product of censorship was the development of a kind of league table of suffering in provincial cities. Days before the terrible raid of November 24, when the shopping centre and Park Street were hit, films of the destruction of Coventry had been shown in Bristol cinemas. But Bristol's big raid received no similar publicity, and this caused jealousy. (In fact, in terms of total blitz casualties, Bristol came sixth in the 'league' with 1,159 deaths, fewer than London, Liverpool and Merseyside, Birmingham, Clydeside and Coventry, but more than Manchester and other major cities.)

As it turned out, the West's newspapers could have been a source of information to the enemy; copies were regularly put on the civil aeroplanes that flew out of Whitchurch aerodrome on the Lisbon run to neutral Portugal. These planes secretly carried VIPs, royalty, heads of state and even film stars, and were much used by foreign agents on both sides.

Another means of keeping up morale was through propaganda: newsreels, films, plays, books, magazines and newspapers were vetted to see that they portrayed a Britain that was brave, cheerful, hard-working, and optimistic.

Given this efficient propaganda and censorship machine, it is not surprising that a rather one-sided image of the West's war emerged, a stiff upper lip, hearty we-can-take-it view that persist-

'It's that Man again', Tommy Handley's ITMA, a surreal response to the frustrations of war. *Left to right:* Tommy Handley, Fred Yule and Jack Train

ed for some years afterwards. It was not until 30 years later, when classified secret documents became available, that Home Intelligence and Mass Observation reports revealed another darker side to the way people thought and felt.

Though people did take all the propaganda, from both the British and the German side, with a pinch of salt, it was nonetheless very effective: it made people think in clichés, and it managed very quickly to mythologise the war.

WINTER IN THE SHELTERS

CHAPTER FIVE

The winter of December 1940 to January 1941 was a cruel one: sub-zero temperatures had to be coped with in damaged homes that had little or no heating and were patched up with tar paper and tarpaulins. Coal was short, food was short, and the poor could not always afford to buy the meagre rations available. There were power cuts and water cuts. It was Christmas and life was miserable.

The memories are of fear, fatigue and, above all, of cold. Bill Graves was one of tens of thousands of Bristolians who suffered the deprivations of surviving one of the worst winters on record in a damaged home.

> The cold was really numbing, it was debilitating. It pulled you down. My grandparents had been bombed out and they were living with us. Their bomb had fallen fairly close to us so all our windows were out. We had bits of tar paper whacked in – unless your roof was off, nobody bothered, you had to soldier on. The wind blew through the tar paper and through every crack and crevice. Coal wasn't easy to come by, so where they'd pulled the wooden blocks up out of the road we'd gather them in a sack or on a cart and take them to burn at home. I remember seeing dozens of people with cars full of old blocks. They had nothing else to burn.

> Our house had its windows blown and the front door blown and we didn't see anybody official. You sent in a card to say your house was damaged and eventually they sent someone to look, officials from the ARP, and they'd write down details on a sheet of paper. People got fed up with how long it took, and the cold... and everything else.

Tess Broughton had equally bitter memories of those January days:

> There was a blitz and we were without heat and water for about two weeks at our home in Bishopston. You just shivered or wrapped yourself well up in what you could find, blankets and things like that. Coal was hardly available, and we were starving. We just didn't get enough to eat and you never saw a fat woman during the war. Then we had an open fire and we used to cook on that and on a little sixpenny meths stove. But there was no water for bathing

A Christmas party in the crypt of St Paul's, Southville for 130 children whose homes
were damaged in one blitz

or anything like that. We did cope until everything was put back on.

The poor suffered especially badly in a Bristol disrupted by repeated blitz attacks. Betty Screen's family survived on the charity of neighbours in the worst times:

> We had bread pudding, we had the ends of loaves that neighbours didn't want, they sent that up. And large tins of baked potatoes – that was the favourite, when neighbours sent over large tins of baked potatoes.

> There was one time we sat down and cried. Mum told us that she was sorry, but there was no food for us. And suddenly a knock would come at the door and it might be half a loaf. So Mum used to cut it into very large, thick fingers and we used to suck the bread to make it last. I know it sounds incredible but that's what we actually did. We used to suck the bread to make it last before we went to bed.

Bill Graves:

> They brought Churchill down with some of the top officials of the Corporation and he went to various parts where bombing had taken place. They came to where I lived and they gathered up the school kids from the local schools like St. Gabriel's and gave them flags to wave. There was such hostility from some of the women who lived near John Street where they'd lost friends and relatives that one of the women went and snatched things away. The police got quite upset about this. She was snatching flags and when Churchill actually turned up the women turned on him, became very hostile and started booing and shouting abuse at him.

> Not only were they very tired, not only were they fed up with the bombing but they were also very, very hungry. Many people were living better as far as food was concerned than they'd been living before the war, but there were still people who couldn't afford to buy rations. With their already deteriorating health there was malnutrition, and that made people tired and irritable and this manifested itself on that occasion. People couldn't bottle it up any more and Churchill was the focal point.

The severe cold of the first half of January increased the difficulties of fire-fighters, rescue parties and repair gangs. It immobilised the turntable ladders, and blow lamps had to be used before they could be set in motion again. Great icicles that hung from roofs and ladders obstructed the fire-fighters and were a menace to those who passed below. The clothing froze on the firemen's bodies so that they were encased in ice and movement of any kind became difficult. If the water pressure failed for a moment, and it often failed at this time, the hose pipes were turned into solid tubes. Pumps were continually frozen and the roads were sheets of ice. The movement of vehicles was slowed up or stopped altogether when speed was essential. For many hours after raids men and women were pinned down under the rubble of demolished buildings, often in great physical pain, with streams of icy water pouring over them.

The 12-hour ordeal of the fourth great attack on January 3, 1941, was followed by another raid the following evening, but this did not develop into a full-scale blitz. Fires broke out in Avonmouth and Bristol and the cold made fire-fighting doubly difficult. Bill Morgan was called out at 4.00 a.m. to deal with a blaze in Victoria Street, near the Shakespeare public house.

> The hoses were all along the gutters and they were frozen solid. You just couldn't move for ice and everything was festooned with icicles. Your clothing got frozen up. I got my fiancée to knit me a blue balaclava and I put that on and put the steel helmet on top of that and the balaclava froze to my face – it was like a solid piece around my face.

The raid in January took place on a bitterly cold night and produced some strange scenes. Two hoses could be seen side by side, one in flames with the firemen at work on it, and the other hung with long icicles where the streams of water had splashed and frozen. The brave and spirited women of the Women's Voluntary Service, taking their canteens out under the bombing with refreshments for civil defenders, had their own troubles that night: the firemen put the cups with dregs down and they froze. The tea froze. The hose froze. 'We had a choice of being frozen, blown up or drowned in tea,' said one helper.

These hazards of deep winter were additional to the normal ones which affected all who had to move about in the blitz – hidden craters, dark lumps of débris, tangles of firemen's hose, and trailing telephone wires. Messengers, ambulance drivers and the WVS had to learn a new technique of locomotion. One WVS driver used to take her student sons out with her in turn. They lay along the bonnet of her canteen taking

Victoria Street in ruins

soundings and calling back to her as she moved forward.

The cold and the shortages and insanitary shelter life were also having an effect on health. The Medical Officer of Health for Bristol found that air-raids affected hygiene. The usual bedtime bath was forgotten on most occasions and the significance of this was not apparent until children were examined for evacuation. Approximately 15 per cent (3-20 per cent of the population, according to locality) were found to be infested with head lice.

There was a big increase in scabies and impetigo, due to shelter life and changed habits in the home: from 200 per year before the war, the number of cases rose to 9,000 in 1942.

Winston Churchill's visit, 1940

After each serious enemy attack, the population was instructed by poster, loudspeaker van, and through the various civil defence services, about the boiling of water and the precautions that should be taken when water was stored in baths, buckets or other receptacles. In spite of all this publicity, some people, too lazy to go to the proper places for their water supply, or too stupid to listen to the instructions they were given, persisted in drinking from fire hoses. As this water was in most instances pumped direct from the river they were fortunate if they received nothing worse than a bad taste in the mouth.

Then there was the vexed question of the air-raid shelters. Could they be trusted?

As Professor Charles MacInnes wrote in *Bristol At War*:

> While the majority of citizens used their cellars, or a strengthened room, or
> were content with a couple of chairs or a mattress under the stairway, a few
> of the richer and more resourceful ones had deep dug-outs constructed in their

gardens, which they furnished with bunks, oil stoves, candles, emergency rations, tables and chairs. In some of them there were carpets on the floors, books and periodicals, and even a picture or two on the walls. At least one prosperous Bristol citizen found that in such a place life could be made quite comfortable even though the city burned. Many did nothing at home but depended for their security on nearby public shelters while not a few dismissed the whole subject with a shrug of the shoulders and the fatalistic reflection that if a bomb was marked for them it would reach them whatever they did, so why worry?

When war was declared, Bristol was in a pathetic state of unreadiness. Only 50 of the 200 ambulances needed were available – at one critical stage, ambulance staff at Easton were told to collect the dead in dust carts. They refused to do so. The city had just 3,500 shelter places ready, though the Home Office calculated that places for 25,000 people were needed.

Moreover, the shelters that had been built were mainly surface structures, brick-built rectangles with thick concrete roofs. No one trusted them, quite rightly as it turned out, for an error had been made by the Ministry of Home Security in the formula for mixing the mortar. If a bomb had fallen on one of these shelters, the bricks would have collapsed, and the occupants would have been crushed by the concrete slab on top. The one in Dowry Parade, Hotwells, collapsed even before it could be used, and the supporting arch gave way in a shelter in Bedminster.

These defective shelters were duly dismantled – they fell like packs of cards – and new ones built, but by then no one had any faith in them.Because these shelters were despised, they were vandalised, used as urinals and refuse tips, and covered in graffiti – 'We want bomb-proof shelters' was a common one. In May 1940 the Emergency Committee was told that damage to shelters at Wedmore Vale, Melvin Square, Bedminster Down and Eastville was so bad that they would be ineffective and probably dangerous in an air-raid.

Mass Observers in Bristol collected comments on the shelter provision: 'It's wicked, having the worst raids in the country and having no proper underground shelters.' 'There's no excuse for not having proper shelters.' 'It's a waste of money to go on building those doll houses' (brick shelters). 'Deep shelters have got to come before the end of the war. It's going to drive people scatty unless they have them.' 'We won't win the war unless we have underground shelters for everyone.' 'It's buggery in them' (surface shelters).

MO also visited shelters and reported that many of the trench type were unusable because they were under two feet of water. 'It's a waste of time to build them, nobody uses them', and 'It's just like our Council. They always realise their mistakes about ten years too late', were comments overheard.

After the first serious raid on Bristol, there was an outcry about the shelters, and a demand that tunnels should be dug into Bristol's seven hills.

The poorer folk flocked to the communal surface shelters, but these quickly lost their reputation as safe refuges when bombs began falling. And for the very good reason that they offered precious little protection if a bomb fell close by. It wasn't long before many people had heard of incidents like the one Bob Chappell witnessed after bombs fell on Bedminster:

> We used to have surface shelters in the streets for local people. On that occasion, I could see that the roof of this shelter had shifted about, well, let's say a foot. It wasn't on square and when I looked inside it was full of people sat side by side all the way round and everyone was dead. They had their eyes open and it was just as if they were sitting there not seeing anything. It was the blast from the bomb. It hadn't affected the shelter, only shifted the roof, but the blast killed them.

The deeper the safer, that was what people began to believe, and it became an obsession. It was as if the city wanted to burrow further and further underground to hide from the horrors above. People hunted out refuges wherever they could, in spite of official warnings that many of the so-called 'safe' places could prove death traps if they suffered a direct hit from an HE.

At one point it was estimated that about 110,000 people were unable to stand the strain of the bombing raids. The stress on Bristol children was great, because there had been no early evacuation of Bristol pupils because the area was considered safe. Teacher Miss G. Wensley took the children in her class down to the shelter:

> In my own shelter on another occasion 30 of us, still children under 6 (except

A shelter party in Bedminster

my 'helper', who was 8), experienced Bristol's first great daylight raid. We had been having solos by varied children when the guns became so very loud (and remember we had never really heard them before) that I decided that community singing was our best remedy. For half an hour we raised the roof with every popular song we knew, going back over them again and again rather than pause for a second. In that thirty minutes – which seemed like a century – I watched 30 little faces go whiter and whiter, and 30 pairs of eyes fill with horror and fear. But their little voices never faltered – no one cried or called out. They grinned as they sang right to the bitter end. We went home speechless from our efforts, but we'd seen that first daylight raid through, and we had learned how Bristol children could and would 'take it'.

The disused Clifton Rocks Railway was another strange shelter. The BBC had taken over part of it, as had BOAC, but the top end was adapted for a public shelter, with each family perched on a series of concrete steps: 'It was very wet and smelly, you had to sit away from the walls to keep dry.' 'We had concerts and fancy dress parties there, it was a real social centre.'

Redcliffe caves were another refuge, but hardly a safe one. 'Very dreary, we squatted where we could. The Vicar used to come to say prayers.' When bombs demolished Redcliffe Infants' School, a crater actually penetrated right down to the cavern below.

Railway tunnels where trains were still running were another risky form of shelter: Ashley Down tunnel was used, as was the railway tunnel that runs by the Portway under Sea Walls. 'We sheltered in a hole in the river bank, and when the alert went we ran into the tunnel. If a train came, we stood in the alcoves with our faces to the wall, so the train drivers wouldn't see and report us.'

The tunnel under the railway at the end of Mina Road was also fully used. 'People brought mattresses and sofas, there must have been 150 of us on the pavement each side. We couldn't use the road, traffic was still going through. It was better than a sur-face shelter: the one in Mina Road park was demolished by a bomb and all inside were killed.'

A small cave up in the rock ten feet above Bridge Valley Road held 12 people – 'There was a special knock to get in' – and the cave below the end of Windsor Terrace was a shelter too, though luckily it was not until after the war that some of the roof fell in.

The old ice house behind Colston Boys' School, on the banks of the River Frome at Stapleton, was another choice; and, perhaps strangest of all, a few sheltered beside the Frome, where it runs underground beneath the heart of the city. 'My uncle was Keeper of the Frome, and he took family and a few neighbours down some steps to the tow-path by the river, under the city streets.'

Blaise Castle House's cellars were an official shelter and so was a tunnel that leads from the house to Blaise Hamlet; crowds went to another, long tunnel below Wills-bridge Hill: 'Damp and smelly, we spent whole nights there, 6.00 p.m. to 6.00 a.m., for months.'

The bonded warehouses in Clift House Road were also used, and so was a tunnel in

The entrance to the improvised shelter in the Portway Tunnel where up to 3,000 would turn up to fight for a place

Queen's Avenue, next to the old Embassy cinema; the crypts of churches were popular, though risky; when fire broke out in St. Michael's Church, the 300 people in the crypt below had to flee for their lives, and a number sheltering in the crypt of St. Barnabas lost their lives when the church was bombed.

The civil authorities were worried by this passion for unorthodox deep shelters and, to do them justice, they had good reason. They had no evidence that these caves and tunnels would withstand a direct hit, and the City Engineer feared that hundreds of tons of rock or brick falling on to a big crowd would cause terrible casualties. They discouraged people from sheltering in large numbers because the potential death toll would be so great.

But Bristolians were obstinate: they said they only felt safe when 'buried in rock'. Attempts to shift them from these refuges were ineffective, and nowhere more so than in the Portway tunnel, scene of the worst public confrontation of the whole Bristol Blitz. It was here that a veritable battle broke out among the civil authorities, the Regional Commissioner and the people. It ended with a sit-in, a visit from the police, a sacking, and telegrams to Buckingham Palace.

When the war started in earnest, people remembered the tunnels that had been built in the rock of the Avon Gorge for the defunct Port and Pier Railway. These had been sealed off when the Portway was built.

There was one long disused stretch, 525 feet long, running under Bridge Valley Road, and a local committee was formed to petition for its opening and conversion into a shelter.

The first shelterers took possession in November 1940. They had failed to persuade the Corporation to make any improvements, and conditions were atrocious.

An Anderson shelter doing service as a coal-house. In wartime, the shelters were erected in holes dug in a back garden, covered in earth, and made as cosy as possible for a family's nocturnal visit

Gerald Smith recalled:

> We thought we'd be the only ones going there. So we trekked down from our house at about 4.00 p.m. It was a dark, cold, winter evening. We got down to the tunnel and there must have been 700 or 800 people. It was absolute chaos. Everyone was trying to get to the tunnel... fear had now taken over because the bombing was so dreadful. We didn't arrive first – we probably arrived almost last. And because we were the last, fortunately we were at the end of the tunnel. The others had jam-packed themselves in. It was terrible. They were fighting for places.

> You couldn't lay out. You stood or knelt, cooped up with your back against the wall, and it was always streaming with water. We couldn't sleep. Sleep was almost impossible. Any sleeping was done during the day; either in

school or at home. Because there were no doors, you couldn't close it off, and people would arrive during the night, especially when a raid was taking place. It was sheer panic.

A Mass Observer visited Portway shelter in December 1940.

> There is no sign, but two printed-paper notices with an arrow pointing in. Just inside there is a blast wall of sandbags. As one enters, the stench is overpowering, a mixture of sandbags, urine, disinfectant, sweat and bedding. For about the first 50 yards one has to walk through water two inches deep, over bumps in the ground. On each side, beds are standing in water. Sometimes blankets or an old mac are placed on the mud. This water is spring water and comes from a spring where people fill their kettles. It is a simple business to divert this water out but Bristol Corporation has refused them permission.
>
> Consequently all night long, water is pouring into the shelter like a miniature waterfall. Further along it is drier, and there is the great congestion. About half a dozen families have tent arrangements of sackcloth, thereby ensuring a certain stuffy privacy.
>
> A little over half way along there is another brick wall. Beyond this the walls are whitewashed and bunks four across have been built. The poorest and dirtiest people of them all are using this end. The children are four to a bunk. Lighting is by candles and oil lamps. Some distance from the other end is a brick wall with sackcloth; on the other side are closets labelled M and W. The closets are never empty for more than 30 seconds at a time; they have to serve 1,000 people. There is a stinking tang of chlorine. Beyond is the open air.

On another visit, the observer noted: 'I saw nine cars outside, one of them a 27hp Darracq. The people start coming in at 1.00 p.m. and before blackout there is only room for half the people to sit down.'

Lord Horder, who was head of a committee set up to investigate conditions in shelters, said of the Portway tunnel that it 'deserved full marks for having everything that a shelter should not possess'.

Yet this was the mecca to which increasing hordes of people came night after night: as word got round that this was the safest shelter in the West, as many as 3,000 would literally fight for a place inside, and they came from as far away as Knowle and Filton. It was said that even some bombed-out people from Coventry came there, too. All classes used the shelter: 'People from posh Clifton houses used to turn up and those who looked drab and grubby got in.'

'It was like a stream of refugees arriving: if you didn't get there by 4.30 p.m. to stake your place, you were too late. There was a lot of jealousy about getting a place. I used to think as a child that the shelter people looked like cavemen, sitting there in the dark and the stink.'

Yet a vital social life sprang up, with parties, contests, entertainments, hymn-singing and games. 'Everyone lost their inhibitions, and the most stuck-up often were the most entertaining.'

But in the official view there was room for only 200 people, and the Corporation was forced to act. The reasons for their delay were very suspect. For a start, the Corporation had bomb-proofed other tunnel space on the Portway for storing civic treasures and archives, items from the City Museum and Art Gallery and Corporation records. This in itself caused anger: people felt their lives were considered less important than works of art.

But there was a deeper and more secret reason for the Corporation's reluctance to allow the Portway tunnel to be used as a shelter. Bristol 'war cabinet's plans' against invasion included the use of the tunnel as an emergency broadcasting station, where the BBC would issue emergency bulletins and instructions to the entire South-west region. This was the real reason for wanting to keep the shelterers out.

The one respectable reason the Corporation had for objecting to the tunnel's use was that the City Engineer believed it to be unsafe, and the Medical Officer thought it was insanitary and a danger to health. Once again the authorities concluded that communists were at the root of a campaign to discredit surface shelters.

The whole affair went right to Cabinet level. In January 1941 the Regional Commissioner, Sir Hugh Elles, wrote to explain the situation to Herbert Morrison: 'Upwards of 1,500 persons had formed a sort of gypsy encampment in this indescribable place and filled it with beds, little shelters and a widespread collection of junk of all sorts,' he wrote. 'It is probable that we may have to take drastic measures and be drawn to forcible eviction.'

Nearby Bath suffered, too, as this dejected group depicts

From the end of November the Corporation was planning to evict all but 200 people, who would be given tickets to gain entrance, but the deadline was endlessly extended because of the outcry this caused, and also because the police said they would not use force if the shelter marshals failed to persuade people to leave. All through December and January repeated attempts were made to get people to leave, but after the heavy air-raids of January 3 even more people turned up, and the authorities feared a mutiny if an eviction was attempted.

Meanwhile the BBC were ready to move in, and on January 1 they lined up wagons full of equipment on the Portway. The 800 occupants staged a sit-in: the women and children stayed in the tunnel all day, instead of going home as they usually did; the police arrived, decided against forcible eviction, and the BBC wagons had to leave.

The occupants of the tunnel organised a counter-offensive: telegrams were sent to Herbert Morrison and to the King and Queen, and deputations went to the Corporation; in the Public Record Office there are several pathetic letters to the Queen from shelter users, saying that they were 'suffering from nerves' and would not feel safe in the shelters offered as alternatives at Blaise cellars and the Clifton Rocks Railway. 'These places do not give the sense of complete burial.' Many sufferers from nerves persuaded their doctors to sign certificates saying they needed to be allowed to stay in the tunnel.

At last the Corporation agreed to carry out a proper conversion of the tunnel, to make it more waterproof and install bunks, and to provide proper sanitation and ventilation. But this would be done if the number of official shelterers could be restricted to 200.

It was only thanks to the persuasive powers of St. John Reade and the shelter committee that eventually, on January 24, the excess population moved out peacefully, limiting the occupants to 200. Sir Hugh Elles wrote a cynical note to Herbert Morrison: 'The redundant population together with their goods and chattels has been winkled out. A few tears but no real trouble. The matter has been very skilfully conducted.'

By April 14, all the official 200 shelterers were moved out, in order to clean the tunnel thoroughly and carry out conversion and improvements, costing £4,257. Typically there was even a row about this for expenditure of only £3,703 had been approved. An unsympathetic Elles telegraphed Morrison: 'All Portway users to clear out. Invalid and nerve cases with no means of transport elsewhere offered alternative accommodation eight and a half and two miles away. The remaining malcontents can accommodate themselves where they can.'

It was one of the most ignoble episodes of the Bristol Blitz, and the memory still rankles. Even now, however, some people remember that dismal tunnel with affection. One man who sheltered there as a child says: 'That place ought to have a plaque on it. It saved hundreds of lives.'

If there was no more room in the Portway tunnel, people soon found underground alternatives. Old pit workings in east Bristol were a magnet to many local people who showed a pathetic belief in their safety. A direct hit would almost certainly have buried any shelterers in tons of choking coal dust, slack and rock, too deep for any rescue operation. Schoolgirl June O'Connor took nightly refuge in a disused coal train tunnel near her home:

> The sirens would start and Mum would get us ready with a bottle of water and
> bread and jam and our coat or blanket and perhaps a pillow and off we would

go. People came from miles around and you'd see them scurrying through the tunnel to get to their favourite place which they'd probably had for weeks and weeks. We would feel terribly cold as we lay down with our coats over us, but we would hear the guns at Purdown and all the bombing above us.

We were cold and frightened so all the strangers used to comfort us and sometimes cuddle us and they would sing songs to try to cheer us up and to help pass the night away. It was really cold. But because there were so many people crammed in this tunnel, it sort of contained our body heat. The walls were terribly damp and you could see the fungi on the walls and the water dripping down. In the morning we would emerge from the tunnel and collect the shrapnel that had fallen. It was a sort of trophy. I can remember going to school and falling asleep on my desk because we had had so many broken nights' sleep. I don't think the teachers minded too much because everybody around us had experienced the same sort of restless nights. We just accepted it, we just thought it was a way of life. It was just something that went on and on.

Throughout this period the voluntary welfare workers and other services set a remarkable example with their help and their cheerfulness. They couldn't keep the bombers away but they could – and did – do their best to help restore crushed spirits as Christmas approached. There was food for shelterers, assistance for the homeless, immediate, practical help for the direct victims of the raids. People responded to their example and whenever, for example, the Red Cross made appeals for blood donors, there was never a lack of willing volunteers. Things even began to improve in some of the worst shelters and Christmas night wasn't the miserable occasion it might have been.

Gerald Smith recalled:

It was better in the Portway tunnel. We even had a Primus stove and could cook a little meal. And people were very genuine. You could leave everything where it was and nobody touched it. There was a lot of comradeship. We all got to know one another, we'd have a singalong.

But the fear was that we were going to have a raid on Christmas night. People would say that the enemy wouldn't do that; there were people saying the enemy would. This apprehension marred Christmas to start with. We went down the tunnel early Christmas Day because it was dark at 4 o'clock. We

The WVS did many jobs: manning rest centres and clothing depots, driving mobile canteens and serving hot food

decorated as best we could, we made some paper chains and put them on the wall. Of course they all fell down because the wall was wet. There were rations for Christmas pudding, so mother boiled up some pudding. I had a little tramways conductor's set. My sister had a knitted doll and I had a comic and we thought it was fabulous. And then people started swapping. If you hadn't got any nuts, somebody else gave you some and if you didn't have any cake, somebody gave you and you gave and they gave.

In Bristol's orthodox and unorthodox shelters that bitter winter, a new comradeship was born.

An ARP Warden searches below perilously balanced masonry on St Michael's Hill

HEROES AND COWARDS?

CHAPTER SIX

No one knows how he or she will react when under life-threatening pressure. Ordinary people find a courage they never knew they had, while others who think they can cope find they are terrified.

During the siege of Bristol, when every citizen was put to the test, a study found that as many as 100,000 people were unable to stand the bombing and were victims of what was then called 'nerves'.

Some were given a nickname: the Yellow Convoy. This was the Bristol description of the people who, during the height of the Blitz, left the city every night for a refuge in the countryside.

Trekking, another name for it, was not just a Bristol phenomenon. When the big raids started, people in Coventry, Plymouth and Southampton did the same. A Liverpool train that left each evening bearing hundreds of businessmen out of the city was known as the Funk Express.

Bristolians of all classes went trekking. The better-off would rent a room out in the countryside and take the whole family there by car each evening. 'You couldn't get a room anywhere for love nor money,' said Ronald Coles, who worked at Bristol Aeroplane Company as a draughtsman.

> We lived on Bedminster Down and every evening we drove off to Failand to a room we rented. We managed to get the petrol because my father was a builder. Every spare room for miles was let out. When my department was evacuated to Clevedon I managed to get a cottage in Yatton for £1 a week. I was earning £4 a week at the time. A controlled rent would have been about 12s.6d.

V.A. Maund wrote in her diary:

> Tues., Jan. 28: Redhill farmer rang us up, to ask if we would like to take two rooms in his cottage, for night refuge, at 25/- a week. I agreed.

> Wed., Jan. 29: Out to see rooms at Redhill. But we have come across a snag

– we cannot leave our Bristol home without a firewatcher on the premises. Also, there is a general feeling of animosity towards those who leave their homes as soon as the sirens go, thus leaving it to the residents who remain to attend to them. The matter is left until Saturday for decision.

To those who wanted to spend the night out of Bristol, farmers let rooms, as did publicans and post-mistresses. 'I went on the train every day, after school, on the Frome line, from Brislington to Clutton, to stay with the post-mistress, and I went back again early in the morning. I was only ten, and it made a very long day for me.'

But petrol was rationed and car ownership was not so common as it is today. The poorer families either clubbed together to run a car, or got lifts on lorries, at one shilling each. The lorries would stop in a country lay-by and the occupants would sleep the night there, in the back of the lorry. Sometimes the passengers were left to sleep in the hedgerows and fields.

Some areas organised coaches to go out nightly to a village where the village hall was used for sleeping, something which caused an upset among the local people. A complaint came to the Town Clerk from a resident of Felton about Bristol people who had come at night and gained access to the village hall without authority. The Clerk to Thornbury RDC complained of the conditions caused by unofficial Bristol evacuees occupying a disused schoolroom, where adults slept at night.

Those who obeyed the Ministry advice to 'Stay Put' were also angry about the trekkers.

'People going out to the countryside were a sore point. They left others to do the firewatching and their attitude was "let their blasted houses burn",' said a former Bristol docker who, with his mates, used to recite jeering verses and boo at the hundreds of people who had left their homes to shelter in the Portway Tunnel.

'There was a lot of ill-feeling; we didn't agree with it, leaving their homes unwatched. People should have looked after their own property.'

'We can tell you of the ones with cars who made their way each night to the safety of the countryside and left it to us to fight fires in the streets where they lived. We were really angry with them.'

People would travel as far as 30 miles out of the city, and the put-upon villagers began

A Red Cross youth group training at Fairfield Grammar School

to feel the strain. In December 1940, Lady Clare Smyth-Piggot suggested that 'more accommodation should be made available in the area of Brockley Coombe for the convenience of persons from Bristol who are making a practice of spending the night there'.

Brockley and Burrington Coombes were popular refuges because of the protection offered by the rocks and caves. V.A. Maund, the Bristol housewife who kept a wartime diary, noted on December 8, 1940:

> Out in the car in afternoon, tea at the Bungalow Café, Burrington Coombe. We saw a large colony of caravans occupied by people who have fled from the city, parked off the Rock of Ages, and the café proprietor told us that cot-

tagers and farmers are besieged by people wanting night accommodation.

Many sleep in their cars along the Coombe and at the side of the road, with tarpaulins and tents. Washing hangs on lines tied to the rocks, and cooking pots and children are scattered around – the colony has grown, and the gorge reminds me of a refugee camp.

A country clergyman in the Brockley Coombe area reported that during December to January, 1940-1941, up to 1,000 strangers had asked for assistance. Some had even come in pyjamas. He had room in his church house for 50. Country people complained that they were disturbed at night by wandering strangers, who knocked at the doors in the hope of finding lodgings.

It is hard to judge how widespread trekking from Bristol was; contemporary commentators compared the nightly exodus to Piccadilly in the rush hour, or a Bank Holiday crowd. A Bristol clergyman with 953 houses in his parish said that 121 were compulsorily evacuated, 80 were voluntarily evacuated, and 235 were left empty at night. In some areas of the city, between 4 per cent and 10 per cent of the population moved out of the city or went out each night.

The Corporation found that even some of its own officers were illegally using their supplementary petrol allowances to trek out into the country.

Another idea was to go out to village pubs at Dundry and Chew Magna, and spend the evening there. If the siren went, they stayed overnight; if it did not, they returned to Bristol.

The authorities were worried by the trekkers, mainly because their homes were left empty at night, easy prey to incendiary bombs which, if not put out, would start fires which could spread to neighbouring property.

So various threats were made, that the ARP wardens would be given the right to break into empty houses, or that homeless families would be billeted there in the owner's absence.

There was a fear of a mass evacuation into the surrounding countryside. The panic and chaos caused in 1940, when France was invaded, and thousands of refugees left their homes to clog the roads was something the British were determined to prevent.

'Stay Put' campaigns were launched, and the vast majority of Bristolians did just that: but it is estimated that at the height of the Blitz some ten thousand left the city every night.

Sir Hugh Elles, the Regional Commissioner, told his superiors at the Ministry of Home Security in a report written early in 1941 that the tendency to 'scuttle' would only be cured by the moulding of public opinion, 'and I suggest very strongly that public opinion must be led by a ministerial pronouncement'. Sir Hugh said that these 'weaknesses' were nasty and dangerous exceptions to Bristol's firm home front morale.

The other side of the coin was the heroism of those who stayed in their fractured burning city, and worked selflessly to save lives. Lord Mayor, Alderman T.H.J. Underdown:

> The full story of the rescue parties will never be told. Many brave deeds were known only to the few participants. The recorded incidents reveal that in one raid alone rescue parties were called to 66 occurrences where they rescued 135 persons alive and recovered many bodies. In another raid their work of rescue involved action at 35 recorded incidents. Often the parties worked feverishly to rescue trapped people. One party tunnelled a ten-foot cutting through the basement wall of a house, and another made a fifteen-foot cutting into a basement from the side of a crater. Often victims were reached by cuts through party walls. Victims were found blown to roofs of adjoining properties. Other citizens, too, gave Trojan assistance. In one instance, two men, one a soldier, fought their way down through the wreckage of a house for five hours because they thought all the occupants would not be dead. In the early morning hours they brought out alive a woman and small boy whose lives had been saved by a brave man throwing himself upon them when the bomb fell.

Tony Riddell at 19 became a volunteer fire-fighter when the bombs fell near his home in Hotwells on January 3. He recalled:

> The law was that any civilians who were not attached to any fire fighting forces had to take cover; some did not but the majority who were at home did. Indeed on that first Blitz the fire-fighting was left to the fire-fighting services. On the second night, however, we were well organised and helped out. All the authorities had fire-fighting units on every rooftop, every battery, every aircraft battery, so were prepared when the firebombs came. If this had been the situation on the very first Blitz, I am sure Bristol would have saved

All hands to the brooms

at least half of the damage.

I said to my Granfer: 'I'm going out to help.' I was 19, strong and robust, and could see the timber yards of May & Hassall well alight in Cumberland Road. The Luftwaffe had done a really good job of catching all of it all right. Houses, shops, too. Bristol had well and truly copped it.

Eventually I reached Cumberland Road, near the huge blaze, where the Auxiliary Fire Service (AFS) was massed, hose pipe upon hose pipe running here, there and everywhere.

I approached a man who looked like a Fire Chief: 'Can I help you in any way?' He replied instantly: 'Thanks, kiddo, not here, but go up to the sugar factory; they badly need help there as they're undermanned.'

I was away and walked down the short road to the big sugar factory, which was roaring and blazing like fury – more pipes, more firemen, more activity, more destruction.

I soon located the man in charge, again I offered my help. 'Go up there, son,' he said and pointed to a lone fireman directing a huge water jet into the flames. 'Relieve him, will you? And tell him to join the others.' The lone fireman said: 'Good on ya, kid; here take this hose and keep it on the centre of that column coming up from the sugar.' I eagerly grabbed the hose while he added the instruction: 'Keep it going into the flames ALL the time.' Then he was gone and I was left there uninitiated and certainly the newest recruit the AFS had got that night.

My jet of water shot up into the sky and downwards into the flames. Pointless it seemed to me, but I'd offered so I thought to myself – let's get on with it, THEY could do it, so why not me?' All through that seemingly long, long night I fought the flames – then I suddenly realised I was very very wet. It didn't matter all that much, now and again I'd wriggle the jet of water at first in little circles, then big circles, across and up and down even 'signing' my name but always, as my instructor had said, into the flames. Eventually, I felt the usual things like tiredness – 'God, isn't there a cuppa about?' – and in the approaching dawn 'Where is my relief?' But still I went on pouring water into the flames with the hose pipe, which by now I'd sort of got quite attached to.

More names 'in water', then he came – the fireman in charge – 'Ere's yer relief coming, kidder. Now go on 'ome and get yerself dried off, your're a good 'un.'

I slouched home, soaked and soggy. The timber yards were still blazing, smoke hung everywhere. People were out on the streets and when I saw Granfer he was worried. 'I'm sorry, Granf, but I've been helping the AFS up Cumberland Road,' to which he replied – as only he could: 'Yer, you get they wet things off and come and 'ave some breakfast.'

Many brave deeds like these went unrecorded and unrewarded, but several Bristolians

Broadmead: firefighting at dawn after a night raid

did win medals for bravery. The following stories were published in *Siren Nights*, a record of Blitz experiences made at the time.

One of the most unusual gallantry awards cases of the war is that of Mr. Henry Cox, 64-year-old member of a Rescue Squad.

Mr. Cox was awarded the British Empire Medal for the courage and enterprise he displayed on a night in November 1940. A direct hit by a high explosive bomb had completely demolished a four-storeyed house at Kingsdown that night. When the Rescue Squad arrived there, the cries of a woman were heard coming from under the débris in the middle of the basement floor. As bombing was still going on, and the risk of falling débris was very great, it was going to be a difficult job to get to her. After a preliminary survey as to her position, Mr. Cox worked his way down through a small opening and found the poor woman buried up to her neck. A bucket was carefully lowered to him, and he proceeded to remove the rubble surrounding the woman with his bare hands, loading it into the bucket again and again. For an hour and a half he worked, all the time talking and singing to the trapped woman to keep up her spirits until at last he was able to lift her sufficiently clear to enable her to be rescued.

Two Sisters from the Bristol Maternity Hospital, Elsie Stevens and Violet Frampton, were each awarded the George Medal for the work they did during a severe raid on the city in March 1941.

Shortly after the alert sounded that night, a call was received at the hospital requesting assistance for a woman about to have a baby. Sisters Stevens and Frampton immediately volunteered to go out, and found their journey a perilous one; bombs were falling and dislodged masonry added to the risks of passage through the streets. On arrival at their destination, they found that their patient was trapped with several other people in the cellar of a house which was in a very dangerous condition. Circumstances were so bad, the raid being at its height, that it had been found practically impossible to continue rescue operations.

Sister Stevens was lowered through a grating, and by lying flat was able to reach one victim. Her difficulties were increased by the fact that the only light available was that given by a torch. However, with the assistance of Sister Frampton and the rescue party, an old lady and two children were released and passed through the grating to safety.

As the pregnant woman was found to be completely buried under débris, Sister Frampton went back to the hospital to obtain morphia. When she returned, Sister Stevens was again lowered into the cellar in order to give the patient an injection. By that time conditions were so dangerous that rescue work overhead had to be suspended. There was all the time a grave risk of the whole building collapsing owing to blast and the shaking of the débris. Nevertheless, the two Sisters went down again and stayed beside their patient, and by 3.00 a.m. they had managed to release her head. They were then able to make her more comfortable, and sustained her with sips of warm tea. All through the night they remained with her while the rescue party worked to clear a way out.

At about 8 o'clock it was thought necessary to call a doctor. He answered the call immediately and went down into the cellar, staying with the Sisters, all three of them doing what they could for the patient in the very awkward and dangerous circumstances until they were finally released at one o'clock in the afternoon, when the patient was taken to hospital. Soon afterwards it was reported that mother and child were doing well.

It is pretty certain that most people have thought at one time or another during an air raid: 'Will they get the gasholder this time?' During a heavy raid on Bristol in November 1940 two incendiary bombs fell on the top of the gasholder at St. Philip's. Without hesitation, Mr. G.D. Jones, the gasholder attendant, climbed the 70 feet to the top, and knocked the bombs off with his steel helmet before they had burnt through the plates of the holder. He was aware at the time that the holder contained over two million cubic feet of gas.

During the same raid the holder was punctured several times by pieces of bomb splinter and flying shrapnel. Each time he heard the sound of escaping gas, and although the raid was at its fiercest, Mr. Jones climbed up and stopped the holes with clay, thereby averting the danger of fire.

On another occasion, the gasholder was badly punctured and caught fire. Although Mr. Jones was not on duty that night he immediately went to the scene of the fire, and it was chiefly due to his efforts that it was put out before any serious damage was done.

For his courage and devotion to duty Mr. Jones was awarded the George Medal in May 1941.

Another George Medallist whose portrait has been painted for the Nation's War

Records is Mr. Herbert Stanford, a Group Warden, who, in November 1940, was instrumental in saving the lives of several people who had been trapped in a bombed house near Redcliff Hill.

While wardens were evacuating the residents of adjacent houses, cries were heard coming from beneath the blazing débris. A fire pump was quickly brought to the scene and, while water was being played on the fire, Mr. Stanford worked his way through to the victims on his stomach and was able to give them some water while he spoke encouragingly to them.

'All Clear'

It was found impossible to get the trapped people out alive by removing the débris on top, and so it was decided to make a hole in the wall which divided the shattered building from the next house. Unfortunately, when this had been done it was still found impossible to get through as there was an obstruction by débris inside. Mr. Stanford, however, was not to be beaten and decided a way could be cleared by knocking out a fire grate. This was an awkward task but it was achieved and it was effective; five people were brought out and taken to hospital. All this took three hours to accomplish – three hours during which the building was still burning, coal gas was escaping, and the raid was still going on. The Lord Mayor, Alderman Underdown, paid tribute:

> Those who have fallen have paid the supreme sacrifice for the honour of the city. Bravely did these valiant hearts bear themselves. Many heroes fell in the act of duty and service for their fellow men, with no thought of self, but bravely carrying on their work of protection and rescue... Our praise cannot be too high, our gratitude cannot be too deep.

Prime Minister Winston Churchill added his praise:

THE PRIME MINISTER'S
MESSAGE TO BRISTOL

The Prime Minister has sent the following letter to the Lord Mayor of Bristol (Alderman T. H. J. Underdown).

10 Downing Street.

My Lord Mayor,

My thoughts have been much with the inhabitants of Bristol in the ordeal of these last weeks.

As Chancellor of the University, I feel myself united to them by a special bond of sympathy, and I have heard with pride of the courage, resolution, and patience with which they have answered these detestable attacks on their families and their homes.

It is the spirit such as theirs which makes certain the victory of our cause.

Yours very faithfully,
WINSTON S. CHURCHILL.

HANGING ON   FEBRUARY TO APRIL 1941

CHAPTER SEVEN

In mid-January the raids died away and the terrible winter lost its grip.

But the raiders returned now and then; on January 16 bombs fell on Ham Green Hospital, where, reported the *Evening Post*: 'Nurses, doctors, porters, the clerical staff all worked heroically for several hours to smother bombs and fight the fires. They clambered on roofs and kicked the bombs into the grounds. They swarmed among the rafters and checked the flames before they could spread. Even some of the patients insisted on leaving their beds and going out in the bitterly cold night.'

There were further light raids in February, the major one being an attack on East Bristol on the night of February 26, when W.A. Hares noted:

> I then look out, and think that I shall see the whole neighbourhood on fire. But all the fires are well under control now, and have been 'outed' successfully. It was some darn good practice for all of us, and I feel proud the way my crew dealt with the situation. There is no doubt that if any one of us had funked it the whole building would have gone up, as we had no assistance from outside.
>
> Planes were still over, but it seemed that the raid had fizzled cut and an early All Clear gave us a chance of looking back on a job well done.

The respite was short. On the night of March 16, Bristol suffered its fifth blitz. The target was Avonmouth and Bristol docks but, although the targets were industrial, the worst damage was in the suburbs, hitting Fishponds, Eastville, Whitehall, Easton, St. Paul's, Montpelier, Kingsdown, Cotham, Redland and Clifton. Of all Bristol's major air attacks this seven-hour raid was perhaps the worst. Poor visibility over the target area meant the raiders drifted over mainly residential areas, being attracted by the fires they had started. The 164 crews of the Luftwaffe reported dropping 164 tonnes of high explosives and 33,840 incendiaries, and the casualty figures in the city that night were the highest of the war, with 257 killed and 391 injured.

Some of these probably died as the result of a premature All Clear which was sounded at 1.40 a.m. and, although a second Alert was signalled 11 minutes later, people had

Fire-fighters in King Street, next to the Llandoger Trow, April 11, 1941

already started to come out of their shelters, only to be greeted by falling bombs. No official explanation was ever given for the blunder.

Ernest Smith was among the injured that night. He was caught by the false All Clear, having left home to make his way to Broad Plain to see what he could do to help at the NAAFI. The alarm went again and he made for the nearest Community shelter.

> As I got inside the shelter, round the corner, I heard this bomb screaming down and I went flat on my face. I thought this was it. I couldn't have been unconscious all that long, probably ten minutes, quarter of an hour. And when I came round my head was spinning, my ears were ringing. And I had a wonderful feeling of being alive. I stumbled over bodies. There were about 20 people killed in there. I knew them personally. I spoke to Mr. Osborne who was there, and he said 'My legs are gone,' and I put my arms round his shoulders and we got into the entrance. We found Mr. Stone lying there. He'd been out to make a tray of tea because of the All Clear, and been caught in the entrance, carrying his tray.

Those who survived made their way across the road to a cellar – one of them was Mrs. Stone, who asked if her husband had survived. Ernest Smith couldn't bring himself to tell her he had been killed. Mr. Osborne died of his injuries and Ernest was treated for his injuries and told he was lucky to have survived. He suffered from claustrophobia ever after.

The undaunted W.A. Hares made his report:

> Planes over. Heavy gunfire. Flares, incendiaries, and bombs begin falling almost immediately. Big fire started at Lawrence Hill. Planes are coming in continuously. Seems that we're in for another picnic. Wonder what the night will bring forth.

> The Huns are certainly mixing them well tonight. Not much chance of their missing the town with the fires they have started so early. Nothing happening just around us, so we go to the top floor to see what and where things are occurring. Two or three fires burning to the east and smoke and flames begin to pour from a factory in the Croft. The blue incandescent light of exploding incendiaries can be seen in several different directions, and bunches of chandelier flares are being continually dropped.

Homeless after a raid

Ground defences are firing tracer shells. Barrage overhead provides suitable 'incidental music', interrupted by the scream of high explosives. We get tired of ducking and just anticipate where they are likely to fall. I watch a string of incendiaries bursting as they strike the roofs of Ellbroad Street. They seem to be coursing straight for the factory, and then take a sudden turn across the ruins of Castle Street, where they are quite harmless. Another lot falls straight up Philadelphia Street – explosive incendiaries, this time – and these are followed by a stick of HEs which pass right over the buildings and fall with tremendous explosions in City and Ashley Roads.

Anderson's and the buildings around are now a huge burning mass, but still the Hun has not had enough. A plane comes in very low and right over Kingsdown and Stokes Croft, lets go both heavy explosives and incendiaries. It seemed that the blast of the bombs temporarily smothered the fire.

Planes are easing off now. Gunfire only spasmodic. A lull ensues, and the All Clear sounds.

Another siren wail. Surely Jerry has had enough for one night! But no. The fires he previously started guide him, but this time the bombs seem to be aimed at residential areas. It goes on hour after hour, until you are sickened utterly by the futility and continued hopelessness of it all. You no longer pay any heed when a stick of bombs falls quite near. Though I've been through several blitzes, this is the first time I have actually seen the eruption of flame and débris. It left me with a very queer and helpless feeling. The All Clear sounded, and another memorable night has been safely passed through.

This raid badly affected morale, reported Mass Observation:

A large proportion of people are definitely nervy. Bad talk and general complaints against the war have distinctly increased. The big raid on Sunday, March 16, has done more to upset morale in Bristol than any two of the previous raids put together. People are getting worn out with the continual bombardment in a place where every bomb is a bomb somewhere quite near you and at you. The irregular, sporadic, sudden switching of heavy raids here has a strongly disturbing effect.

Then in April the weather improved, the night skies were clear and the enemy planes returned. On April 3 and 4 they were back, but by then the fire-fighting services were so effective that no big fires developed. Easter was approaching, and Bristolians hoped that, as at Christmas, they would be spared a heavy attack. It was not to be.

On Good Friday, April 11, 153 bombers set out to attack Avonmouth and Portishead docks, and then Bristol. The raid lasted for just over five hours, with 193 tonnes of high explosive and 36,888 incendiaries raining down. The first half of the raid hit the Centre and north Bristol, the second half the Centre, Bedminster and Knowle; 180 people were killed and 382 injured.

Joyce Williams:

We were washing up the dishes when the first bomb that night fell on a nearby road. We heard its whistle before the siren went, and did not have time to get to the Anderson shelter in the garden, so dived under the kitchen table away from the windows. It was one of the longest and most widespread air-raids we had experienced, with a short break around midnight. It was not until daylight that we heard the final All Clear. Once again, we had no water, gas or electricity, but we had a coal fire in the breakfast room. Mother had some-how obtained a small hob, and attached it to a bar of the grate rather precari-ously, but we did manage to boil a kettle of water, or place a saucepan on it. From the first of the night time raids in the November, we had kept the bath, and as many buckets and utensils that we possessed, filled with water. It was a precious commodity in those days.

After breakfast, I started to make my way to the office, past burning build-ings, rescue services still searching for people in the rubble, and seeing an occasional UXB sign.

Miss Fagnani, who lived in Colston Street, wrote in her diary on Easter Monday:

It is a strange and awful Eastertide for Bristol, and the city is full of morbid sightseers, whom I have no time for. All the big papers on Sunday have given us a good write up; they say we have had the worst raid outside London so far, and Bristol is the worst blitzed city of the lot. So if we exist at the end of the war we shall have something to feel proud about for having 'stayed put'. Though I am no church-goer, I believe in God, and through it all I have never lost my faith.

W.A. Hares:

Good Friday: It's very quiet this evening, and we're really not expecting any-thing to happen. The siren goes and we stand by as usual.

In come the planes. The barrage opens up immediately but, unlike the first blitzes, there are now plenty of fire-watchers. Matters are more organised; the novelty of being subjected to aerial bombardment has faded, and we know our own capabilities to deal with any fire bombs that fall in the district.

Unable to see much in the street we go up to the top floor to take a look if anything should happen. It's not a bad view; orange and red flares drift slow-ly down, the red bursts of the ack-ack shells followed by the drifting white

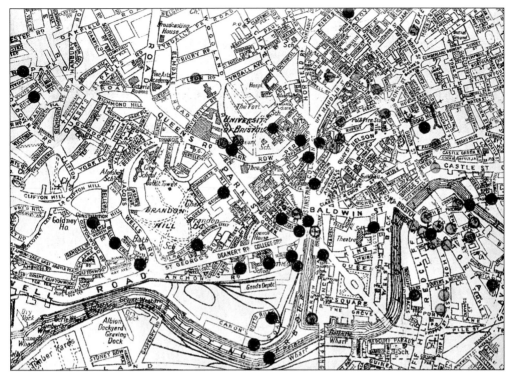

Detail from the original ARP Control Room map showing where bombs fell in the city centre during the Good Friday Raid

halos light the sky whilst we wait for the more vigorous and devastating part of the play to begin.

With a terrific shriek a large bomb falls on Broadmead. Then a string of incendiaries swishes across Cotham and beyond. We watch a series of different lines of incendiaries and applaud or criticise when they are not outed quickly or allowed to take hold. In quick succession five lots are plotted and it is now apparent that Jerry needs more than incendiaries to get the people of this town panicky. In spite of this, there are big fires raging in Cheltenham Road, Stokes Croft and Kingsdown, and it seems that Jerry is determined to increase these.

My mates and I stand looking out of the windows wondering if and when anything is coming our way. Then, in the distance, the blue incandescent light

'Here you are, these ear plugs should do the trick'

of exploding fire bombs is seen down across the roofs and streets starting from the top of the Croft, coming half way down then taking a SW turn towards us. We watch them come nearer – Brunswick Square, Rosemary Street and up the Friars. I shout to my mates to duck under the table, expecting to have the rest right through our own roof.

Seconds pass. We think it's all right now, and one of us suggests we go and look for souvenirs. Coming down the stairs we get a shock. There is our souvenir burning away in the office. Using the now successful method of past raids, I let the bomb have a full bucket of water. Up she goes in a sheet of flame and sparks. Harry comes behind with the sandbags and dumps them on top, and Bert brings up the rear with two more buckets of water. Beyond a little mess no damage is done.

We now go down to the street to see if any more had dropped near. What a difference from the first blitzes when a single fire bomb could do tremendous damage through the lack of training and knowledge! The All Clear goes, and we prepare for a night's rest.

But we have no luck. Off goes Moaning Minnie again, and we get ready for the second half of the show.

The barrage, which had tailed off considerably during the last hour, now opens up again with fresh intensity, and whilst watching the innumerable bursts in the sky we get the surprise of our lives. The great black shapes of a COUPLE OF GERMAN BOMBERS come sailing in well below the balloons. With three guns firing from them at the balloons and the ground defences they pass right overhead, and let their load of hate fall near the Centre.

The attack flow shifts to the middle of the city, and fires spring up in Redcliffe Street, the Centre and Park Street. They quickly get out of hand and become beacons – a guide for far more terrific bombing. A few more incendiaries across Stokes Croft, St. Michael's Hill and Park Row. Big fire starts near gasometer at the back of the Eye Hospital.

Hell let loose again; terrific bomb attack. Fire in Park Street now assumes huge proportions, and flames leap high into the air, reminiscent of the first blitz.

Raid goes on till early morning, by which time the early fires had died down, and I think everybody had had just about enough.

Winston Churchill, the Prime Minister, was due in the city the following day to confer degrees at Bristol University, in his capacity as Vice-Chancellor:

C.M. MacInnes:

The city was still smouldering, and the crash of walls, where the repair gangs were at work, could be heard as the academic procession formed. Hose pipes and other evidences of the night's work lay in its path and pools of water were everywhere on the floors. The room in which the Prime Minister took sherry with the University Senate and Council, before the conferment of degrees began, had been just a few hours before the scene of strenuous fire-fighting for it adjoined the blazing Coliseum.

The speeches delivered were short but eloquent and the Prime Minister was obviously deeply moved:

Here we gather in academic robes and go through ceremonials and repeat formulas – here in battered Bristol, with the scars of new attacks upon it.

Many of those here today have been all night at their posts and all have been under the fire of the enemy, under heavy and protracted bombardment. That you should gather in this way is a mark of fortitude and phlegm, of a courage and detachment from material affairs worthy of all that we have learned to believe of ancient Rome or of modern Greece.

I go about the country whenever I can escape for a few hours or for a day from my duty at headquarters, and I see the damage done by the enemy attacks; but I also see side by side with the devastation and amid the ruins quiet, confident, bright and smiling eyes, beaming with a consciousness of being associated with a cause far higher and wider than any human or personal issue. I see the spirit of an unconquerable people. I see a spirit bred in freedom, nursed in tradition which has come down to us through the centuries, and which will surely at this moment, this turning point in the history of the world, enable us to bear our part in such a way that none of our race who come after us will have any reason to cast reproach upon their sires.

Joyce Williams:

During the morning, a rumour went around that Mr. Churchill was at the University conferring degrees on important people. We could hardly believe it. However, when the office closed at 12.30 p.m. a small group of girls, myself included, though extremely tired, made our way up the steep Park Street to the University. That famous shopping street had been badly damaged again, as had Queen's Road in which the University was situated. In fact, part of the University building had been on fire. Shops opposite were still burning, and firemen and ARP personnel were busily engaged. Other than a couple of policemen on the steps of the University building, there was no sign to indicate that Mr. Churchill was inside. A very small crowd had gathered, and eventually people started chanting 'We want Churchill'. Shortly afterwards, a group emerged from the building, led by Mr. Churchill, and followed by Mr. Winant, the American Ambassador, Mr. Menzies, Prime Minister of New

Three thousand Bristol homes were destroyed and many more damaged

Zealand, upon whom Mr. Churchill had been conferring degrees, Mr. Avril Harriman, an American representative, the Lord Mayor, Sheriff and University dignitaries. Many of the latter had their gowns over ARP or Home Guard uniforms.

At first, Churchill looked over the little knot of people to the still burning buildings, and the scene of desolation all around. We in turn gazed at this short stocky figure, whose radio speeches had so inspired us, despite his promise of blood, toil, sweat and tears, which had become such a reality. What was there about this man which so impressed us and gave us such confidence? I cannot, even nowadays, begin to explain.

Someone shouted for three cheers for Churchill. We raised our voices as much as we could, but it was a thin, ragged cheer from parched throats, dried by the acrid smoke billowing around us. Mr. Churchill took off his hat and looked at us, his gaze coming to rest on our small group. We were only a few feet from him, and I saw the tears in his eyes.

Mr. Harriman later reported that, when returning to London, Mr. Churchill said: 'They have such confidence in me, I cannot let them down.'

By now, Bristolians were worn out. Iris Caple:

Children were upset, they were cold and miserable, getting no sleep. Parents' nerves were getting really ragged. It was night after night without an hour's sleep. Most people were just about fed up with it and saying that it was about time that it was all ended, these wars should never be, that these wars were planned out by heads of state and the people left in the dark. A lot of the older people said they'd had enough. I think a lot were ready to give up.

That mood of despondency had its echoes in most corners of Bristol as the last bombers droned away into the early morning sky on Saturday, April 12, 1941. Bill Morgan put it like this:

I had had about two hours' sleep all that week. That just gets you down. You think, I can't go on much longer, and that was the feeling on that Saturday after the Good Friday raid. The human spirit can bear so much... there's a limit. Everybody was scared at heart. When you had this thing going on and on all night and into the next morning, you dreaded what was going to happen the next evening and perhaps the next after that.

The general feeling I found by talking to people – and I thought the same myself – was that if there had been another raid on the Saturday evening after the Good Friday raid, panic would have arisen in Bristol. I think that would have finished us off in Bristol. The people had just about had enough.

After the Good Friday raid, the blitz which lived longest in the memory of Bristolians, there were a few more shorter and less devastating attacks, and one of them, on May 14, was recorded from the German point of view, by observer Rudi Prasse, as his Junkers 188, one of 91 bombers, flew towards the city:

Gefreiter Rudi Prasse, who wrote the account of the May 14 night attack on Bristol

> As we cross the coast the first searchlight beams flash on: two four, five beams finger the sky, searching. Behind us are many more, certainly about 50: this is the famous English coastal searchlight belt. Then we are through and it is dark again. Before us lies Bristol, our target.
>
> We arrive at the outskirts at 23,000 feet. Suddenly two great tentacles of light swing across the sky to flood the cabin with dazzling blue light, forcing us to screw up our blinded eyes. I hold my map against the nose so that the pilot can see his instruments. We dive through a thousand feet, turning steeply to the left, then fly straight ahead. The two searchlights, which have been joined by a further two, hunt the sky for us but we are once more in darkness. 'Heavy flak coming up,' calls Erich [the central gunner] and Hans [the pilot] immediately changes course. There, above us at 6,000 feet, the first eight shells burst.
>
> More searchlights cut across the sky and the flak bursts multiply. The dance has begun! The pilot flies uncommonly well, improvising an aerobatic programme before our eyes.
>
> To the left and below us a flaming red torch goes down. I note in my log 'Aircraft shot down at 01.42 hours south-west of Bristol'.
>
> 01.45 hours! The first flares blossom in rows over the city, lighting the targets with their bright white glow. Over them hang the rows of green sky markers, which float down slowly. On the ground the flak gunners concentrate their

fire on the markers, in an attempt to shoot them out. But it is too late. On the city heavy bombs are now bursting, and dark red fires rise into the sky.

One short glance at the map – that must be the target there. I nudge Hans and point to the right. 'We will attack.'

Bomb doors open, switches on! There is a small jerk as our bombs fall away. Bomb doors close! Our Dora [the Junkers], lighter by more than two tons, obeys its pilot and sweeps round in a steep left turn, on to a south-easterly course away from the target. Soon we are clear.

Although no one realised it at the time, the Good Friday raid was to be the final saturation raid on Bristol, and the Luftwaffe turned its attentions elsewhere. But there was one final horror to come.

After the last raids of spring 1941, Bristol was no longer in the front line of attack. Wartime life continued drearily, but most Air Raid Alerts were for German planes on their way to bomb other cities. As far as was possible Bristol was getting back to normal when at 9.20 a.m. on August 24, 1942, a lone aircraft, on an experimental high altitude raid, dropped death in the form of a single 500-pound high explosive bomb.

It fell on a car parked in Broad Weir. The blast hit one nearby bus and the contents of the fuel tank were sprayed on two more buses loaded with passengers.

In this massacre, 45 people died, most of them women and children, and 56 were injured.

No siren went, no anti-aircraft guns fired, until after the bomb had fallen and rescue services and fire engines were delayed by rush-hour traffic. The loss of life was extra high because Broad Weir was being used as a temporary bus terminus. In fact the buses were not bombed: they caught fire from the petrol and burning fragments from a private car which received a direct hit.

Yet, miraculously, a few did survive the inferno. Margaret Lowry was upstairs on one of the buses:

> We were just moving off and I was looking out of the window when there was this almighty flash. We didn't hear the bomb because it was too close. Then the blast came, but the bus went on. I was told later that the driver had been

Daylight horror: Broad Weir, August 24, 1942

killed instantly and that his foot was still on the pedal. The blast was like an iron hand in a velvet glove, it kind of tightened you so you thought you were going to burst and then let go, and came back again. After it had passed, I looked at the girl I was with and she wasn't there. I couldn't see very well, it was all dark. I felt the seat and she wasn't there so I got down on the floor and felt around and she wasn't there, and I found someone's head without a body... it was getting hot, the bus had caught fire.

There was a man sitting there and I said come on, and he didn't move, I touched him and he kind of collapsed, so I felt my way to the back of the bus and I found my friend just standing there, looking dreamily into space. I said we've got to get off, and she said yes, we've got to find a hospital to help all these people. And we got off the bus, I don't remember how, maybe we jumped down the stairs, and we ran off in the wrong direction to the hospital. I collapsed by a garage and they came out and took us in there and tried to bandage the wounds. There weren't enough ambulances so I had to go up to the hospital in the back of a baker's van. I thought I was dying. I was cut by shrapnel and glass and my face was all bloody. I remember putting my hand on a white board at the hospital and seeing a bloody handprint. I was bleeding so much that the blood prevented my being burned. I was very lucky.

Ken Simmonds was also at the scene of carnage. He worked at a nearby factory and ran out when the bomb fell:

We all rushed round the corner and saw the three buses, and a gang of us made for one in the middle of the road and started pulling people out as fast as we could. Then the bus caught fire and it started working back to us so we could not stay there very long. Most people were unconscious or dead, one or two were screaming but the trouble was we couldn't get at them, because the bodies were all on top of one another, legs were trapped and the seats were blown over and you kind of had to unravel people to get them out. Then the Fire Brigade arrived and the ambulances and as I was a part-time fireman I gave a hand and got a hose pipe on to the flames.

I saw some terrible sights; one chap had his head chopped off at the scalp. I went around later helping a man count the dead bodies, and in one of the buses I saw the driver, and he'd been killed by the blast and then the fire had made his body swell up like a rice pudding. A dreadful way to describe it but that's what it was like. The memory of that day is rooted in my mind, especially of the man who was conscious and crying 'For God's sake get me out' and we couldn't get at him because of the flames. That evening I went out for a meal and I just couldn't eat it. I took my girlfriend to the pub and, although I'm a teetotaller, that night I bought a pint, to try to make myself sick, to get the horror out of my system.

AFTERMATH

CHAPTER EIGHT

There are few outward and visible signs left of the siege of Bristol. You can find a few walls pockmarked by shrapnel, see the bare ruined churches of St. Peter's and St. Mary-le-Port on Castle Green, the empty shell of Temple Church, and the outline on the ground of the vanished church of St. Andrews, Clifton.

Castle Street, where thousands shopped on a Saturday night, is now covered with grass, and the devastated Wine Street and Union Street area is now rebuilt. The University Great Hall had its ornate timber roof replaced, and it's hard to spot which buildings in Park Street are original and which are copies.

The scale of the destruction and damage is not evident now, but to those who lived through the siege the six blitzes changed the face of the city completely.

A few clues are there if you know where to look. The Llandoger Trow pub in King Street had five gables – now it has three. There is a tram rail embedded in the church-yard at St. Mary Redcliffe. Bristol still has some prefabs, built to house those made homeless by the bombing.

Many streets and much loved old buildings were completely destroyed or left as ruins: the old tightly packed shopping centre on what is now Castle Park, the black and white timbered Dutch House, St. Peter's Hospital (a fine medieval building in the heart of the city), several almshouses, St. Peter's, St. Mary-le-Port, St. Nicholas and Temple churches, much of Park Street, the University Great Hall, the Prince's Theatre on Park Row, and the Coliseum skating rink opposite, Merchants' Hall, several cinemas, including the Regent in Castle Street, the Stoll, Bedminster, and the Triangle in Clifton … The list seemed endless when drawn up at the end of hostilities. The horror of the great loss of life and homes, along with much of the fabric of the old city, was made all the worse because at the time no one could know how long the destruction would last. Would the whole city be flattened?

That was the physical aftermath of the siege. The psychological and social aftermath was more complex and far-reaching. When the lights went out all over the West Country on September 3, 1939, it was goodbye to a different world. The West was still

A much loved landmark, and one of Bristol's greatest losses.
The Dutch House on the corner of High Street and Wine Street

VE Day Celebrations: Thanet Road, Bedminster

smarting from the long haul of the Depression years, of the dole queues and the hated Means Test, and in the rural areas much of farming was still virtually unmechanised and life was hard. It was still a world of rigid social barriers, but one which was beginning to improve for the working class. The worst of the Bristol slums had been cleared and 65,000 people moved to the nine new council estates which ringed the city.

But the poor were still suffering from malnutrition: a Bristol University survey in 1938 found that some 40,000 Bristol families were living in poverty in the city, at a time when it was estimated that a family of man, wife and three children needed 37s. 6d. a week, excluding rent money, to live on. They found that a fifth of the working-class families were unable to give their children a proper start in life, and tests had proved that children in Bristol's state schools were inches shorter and pounds lighter then their

Crowds gather in Corn Street on VE Day

counterparts in the private and public schools.

By the end of the war society had changed, class barriers had broken down through shared suffering. Rationing had improved the health of the poorest, women had discovered new possibilities after being sent out to do the work of the absent men. There was hope of a new beginning, of a welfare state, of a fairer Britain, with better housing, better health, better education.

When the joy of VE day wore off, disillusion set in. The rationing and the queues went on, there were not enough homes, and the flowering bomb-sites seemed to be there for good – a few of them were still there in the 1970s.

Joyce Storey recalled:

The war swept away a lot of mid-Victorian pre-conceived ideas about the roles of men and women. For us it opened up new horizons, and by acquiring new skills we found we could do things we never thought we were capable of doing. We found a new independence and a new self-esteem, we had money in our pockets.

We dreamed of a better tomorrow, a socialist Britain, it was our Utopia. It would give the working-class a bigger slice of the cake and there would be equal opportunities for all.

Bill Graves, later to become a Labour Councillor, shared her views:

I grew up in an area of deprivation, though I wasn't deprived myself, and after the war people said, 'We're not going back to that life, we've stuck the war out and now we're going to have something better.'

It was this feeling that won Labour the 1945 election: it was not so much a vote on the conduct of the war as a verdict on the ten years which preceded it. Joyce Storey remembers the euphoria in Bristol after the Labour victory:

It was like VE Day all over again, people were dancing in the streets and hugging one another. We thought this was it, all we'd dreamed about, the welfare state, free medicine, better housing was all round the corner.

It was going to be the New Britain, we were going to be responsible for our own communities, we were going to have community councils, we would plan our city and set up a task force to build new houses – and it never came to pass.

In fact grim austerity in Britain lasted into the 1950s, as did the rationing and the scarred bomb sites blooming with buddleia and campion. Bristol's recovery from the war, as elsewhere, was slow and painful.

Ask any member of the war generation and he or she will say this: it changed me, and changed my life. On a simple level, the war generated lifetime habits: an attachment to listening to new bulletins, of eating too much bread, of drinking too much tea. The war generation is thrifty and hates waste. They switch off lights, and never waste food, or throw away clothes. They still make-do and mend.

Barbara Stinchcombe, a child during the war, says:

Castle Street in the late 1940s. Much of the area would remain derelict for decades, while the city council dithered over what to do with it

The war made me value people, not things. My husband and I both escaped death – I was due to be evacuated to Canada on *The City of Benares* which was sunk, and my husband and his mother ran for and missed one of the Broadweir buses that was burned. So we both feel our lives are a gift to us. The war taught me to be prepared for disappointments. All through it, I begged my mother for a doll's pram, but there wasn't one to be had, and in a strange way I think this early disappointment taught me to bear the fact that I was never able to have a real baby to push in a real pram. I think the war generation is happier with simple pleasures. It's not the end of the world if you don't get what you want.

But there were adverse effects, too, which came from missed educational chances, separation and childhood bereavements and shattered nerves. Even now, some of the war generation still flinch at the sound of a siren, or a loud plane flying overhead. Moreen Sellars suffered from depression all her life, something her psychiatrist traced back to her terrifying war experiences:

> I do not look back upon wartime with any affection. It has affected me for life. My feeling is that life is short and terribly precious and that everyone should treasure what they have. I always want people to be happy and safe and I get into terrible depressions if there is a death, or a rift in the family. I'm sure this is linked with my experiences in the blitz when I had to be responsible for my family. I cope well in a crisis but I collapse afterwards. I'm full of insecurity and it was the war that caused it.

Young lives were disrupted by having an absent father, a destroyed home, constant changes of school.

Five-year-old Doreen Ramsay was sheltering with her mother in the Anderson shelter in the garden just off Parson Street, Bedminster. A bomb fell just outside the door, blowing the shelter and its occupants over the railings at the end of the garden, and on to the railway embankment. When they were dug out, they found their home was no longer standing.

> For the next four years, until the end of the war, we were like refugees, moving into properties belonging to families who had been evacuated. I spent time in four different houses and went to four different infant schools.

Gladys Locke:

> Every night I used to make a bargain with God: 'Please God, spare me and I will never be miserable again.' It was a wicked thing to do but that's what I actually did. War made you think what a wonderful thing life is, so you used to promise God you'd be an ideal person if you were spared. Of course after the war you almost forgot it all, how everyone had been friendly, fighting in a common cause. I learned, too, that not all Germans were monsters. After the war, we had a pre-fab and we had some German prisoners of war to do our garden. They were the two nicest boys I have ever met. They were so kind,

they made toys for my children. It was amazing. I used to think: 'These same boys were up there bombing us, and we were bombing them,' and yet I was really fond of those two German boys.'

Everyone mourned the lost landscapes of their cities and towns, for so much had vanished for ever. Gerald Smith:

You couldn't take it in; there was the cinema you used to go to, the church you used to go to, your library, gone up in flames. Park Street was a row of twisted girders, Castle Street where we shopped was gone; and even now you still remember the old city that disappeared, and feel a certain guilt that you survived when so much and so many didn't.

Nor were the dead forgotten. Arthur Backhurst, who as a young man survived the raid on BAC at Filton, never forgot his workmates who died:

I always think about them, even now. I have a photograph of the bronze memorial plaque that's in the Filton canteen, and I get it out every now and then and go through all the names, and think about them. There was Mervyn Prewitt and Jimmy Ratchford, George Hill, Arthur Plunkett and Vyvian Roberts... and I feel sad. It was all a long time ago, but yes, you feel sad.